VANNA SPEAKS

Vanna White
with Patricia Romanowski

Foreword by Pat Sajak

WARNER BOOKS

A Warner Communications Company

WARNER BOOKS EDITION

Cover design by Jackie Merri Meyer
Cover photo by Harry Langdon
Designed by Giorgetta Bell McRee

Warner Books, Inc.
666 Fifth Avenue
New York, N.Y. 10103

 A Warner Communications Company

Printed in the United States of America

This book was originally published in hardcover by Warner Books.
First Printed in Paperback: April, 1988

10 9 8 7 6 5 4 3 2 1

This book is dedicated to my mother,
who gave me so much strength and courage.
All I can say is,
"Momma, you made me what I am
and I will love you forever."

ACKNOWLEDGMENTS

Without the love, support and help of many wonderful people, it would have been impossible for me to write this book. My special thanks to:

Larry Kirshbaum, president of Warner Books, for being the first person to believe I had something to say.

Nansey Neiman, Warner's publisher, for her enthusiasm and belief in my project.

Susan White, Warner's personnel director, who came up with the title, *Vanna Speaks*.

The City of North Myrtle Beach, for all the loyalty and support everyone there has given me.

Herbert White, my father, who taught me right from wrong through all these years. I love you.

Peggy Hursey, who I know will always be there for me.

Bob McCoy, a loyal friend who is like a grandfather to me.

Leo and Neva Gibson, for raising such a wonderful son and letting me be part of his life.

Carol and Mike Barnes, for all the good times we shared together with John.

Merv Griffin, for giving me the job on *WOF*. I will be forever grateful to you.

The *WOF* staff, those incredible people behind the scenes that you never see. They work extremely hard and deserve a big hand.

Nancy Jones, who makes all the decisions and runs our show.

Pat Sajak, a good friend who, from the start, made my job so easy and so much fun. Thanks, Pat!

Annette Kizer, my best friend in the whole world.

Ray Manzella, my personal manager, whom I thank for his business wisdom but, more importantly, for his true friendship.

Chip White, my brother, who means more to me than anyone. He's an extension of my mother, and I will always love him as much as I love her.

Jamie Raab, my editor, who was my backbone from the beginning. She made me believe I could write this book even when I was sure I couldn't.

Bart Andrews, who started *Vanna Speaks* with me and pulled out thoughts and memories buried so deep inside me that I didn't even know they were there. Without his endless dedication and hard work, this project would never have come to be. Thank you, Bart.

Patty Romanowski, for her extraordinary writing talent and her uncanny ability to capture the real me.

FOREWORD
by Pat Sajak

It was a dirty job, but somebody had to do it. Somebody had to tape brief interviews with the dozen-or-so lovely young women chosen as semifinalists in the race to be the new hostess on *Wheel of Fortune*. So, as the host, that duty fell to me. It was the autumn of 1982, and Merv Griffin, *Wheel*'s creator, wanted to see how I looked on tape with each of them as well as how we seemed to relate to each other on camera.

The last of the group was someone named "White." Her first name was "Vanya" or "Savannah" or something like that. I mean, who ever heard of a "Vanna"? And she was nervous; I mean *nervous*. Her upper lip quivered and her tiny voice trembled. She was gorgeous and seemed very sweet, but who would hire a bundle of nerves with a name no one could even remember? Merv Griffin, that's who. The rest, as someone (probably Merv) once said, is history.

Today, everyone knows Vanna. In fact, like Garbo and Cher, she needs only one name. Babies, dogs, cats, and at least one street now carry that name. Her face has adorned more magazine covers than the universal pricing code. The demands for her time are so great she considers a five-show taping day for *Wheel* to be a vacation. Her lip no longer quivers, nor does her voice tremble. She has developed into one of the smoothest, most charming ladies on television. Where she once had trouble doing an audition interview with me, she now has correspondents from *60 Minutes* eating out of her hand.

How did it come to all of this? Well, that's for Vanna to tell you, and on the following pages, she will. All I can tell you is that she has been a joy to work with and to be with. She is a friend and a confidante. And amazingly, all of the success and all of the public adulation have not changed her. She is what she seems: kind, sweet, funny, ingenuous, and a bit baffled by what's been swirling around her. As she frequently says, "I'm just a letter turner."

Still, there are millions of males in the country who would love to change places with me—not for the fame or the money or the recognition, but for the chance, just once, to turn their heads and utter those two little words that bring the hostess of *Wheel of Fortune* floating through the curtains. . . .

"Oh, Vanna."

PREFACE

♥

About a year ago, when my publisher approached me to write this book, I wasn't really sure what it would be about. At that time, my life seemed to be going in two very different directions. There was my public life, with *Wheel of Fortune* doing better than ever and me suddenly finding myself in every magazine I picked up. Then there was my private life, and the fact that I was still coming to grips with the recent accidental death of my longtime love, John Gibson. What would I say?

My publisher pointed out to me that I was a woman of mystery, because I didn't talk on the show, and if the amount of fan mail I get and the number of times I get stopped wherever I go is any indication, I suppose people do want to know more about me. When I looked through all my press clippings, I realized that even though a lot has been written about me, it's all been pretty much the same information—true and false. Around that time I saw what seemed to be about the tenth headline about my supposed secret romance with Pat Sajak and how I held occult ceremonies in my living room, and I decided that I'd seen enough. I also thought back on my career and my life. My "overnight success" that you've read so much about actually took over a decade of hard work and tough breaks. And my life before and throughout that is, despite some very tragic moments, really the story of a dream come true. It's a story that I'm very pleased to share with you.

Whenever I'm asked how a letter-turning game-show hostess became the object of what one paper termed "Vannamania," I have to say that I honestly don't know. All I do know is that it happened to me, and it's changed my life in ways that I never imagined it could. For that, I'll always be grateful.

And since I can't talk to each and every one of you personally, I can only go by what you've sent me. For example, since I've been on the show, at least fifteen couples have written to tell me that they've named their baby daughters Vanna, after me. Besides being flattered by the compliment, I couldn't help but think how lucky they'll be to go through life with people knowing how to pronounce their names. For years I was Vonna, Vanya, Vonda, Vayna—you name it.

I'm also tickled to read that some little girl has written to tell me that she's rechristened her Barbie doll Vanna. Having been a big Barbie fan myself, I can appreciate that.

Sometimes parents and grandparents write to me on behalf of kids, like the grandmother who wrote to say her son likes to watch me clap, or a mother who let me know that her little girl liked a certain dress I wore on the show. I've received photographs of a white puppy named Vanna, and of a cat who runs to the television whenever her master calls out, "Vanna's on," and watches the whole show. You might think that's crazy, but I wrote back to the cat. And, of course, I can't forget the Vanna White Fan Club league that bowls every Monday in St. Paul, Minnesota. And each week's mail brings hundreds of more questions.

Now, I can understand how people may not really know all that much about me, personally, but every once in a while I discover that lots of times I don't even really look like the "me" most of you know. Maybe the fact that off the set I usually wear sweats, sneakers, a ponytail, and no makeup has something to do with it. I've been in the supermarket and had people come up and say, "You know, you look just like Vanna White." When I reply that I am, they don't believe me. Another time, a woman came up and said, "You look just like a *young* Vanna White." All I could say was thank you. And several times couples have approached me, and the husband said, "My wife and I have a bet going. I say you're Vanna White, and my wife says you're not." I sometimes wonder if I'll hear a voice saying, "Will the real Vanna White please stand up?"

Well, here I am. And here's the whole story—all truth. I think you'll be surprised to know how much of what you thought was true isn't. In a way, this is really two books. One is to thank all my friends and family, especially my late mother, for their support and encouragement through the years. The other is for all of you who've been such great fans. I'm very happy to share my life with you.

And finally, to answer one of my favorite questions right here at the start: Do I really speak? Sure. After all, I couldn't fill very many pages with just "hi"s and "bye-bye"s, could I? So here it is: *Vanna Speaks*—to you.

1

♥

During the years before I started working on *Wheel of Fortune* in 1982, I was a struggling model-actress with a dream—to one day make it on television. Now that I have made it, it's funny to think back on how I thought it would be and how it really is. Not that I have any serious complaints—in fact, I couldn't enjoy my job any more than I do. But it's amusing to realize that even though I don't have what you would call a typical job, I do have a typical day.

Unless I have to get up early for something special, I usually sleep until about nine in the morning. Every day I get an affectionate greeting from my two little feline roommates, Rhett and Ashley. When they hear the cats' names, lots of people automatically assume that I named them after Ashley Wilkes and Rhett Butler, characters from *Gone with the Wind*. In fact, I named my female Ashley because she's a soft, smoky gray–colored longhair. When I saw her, the name just came to me, and it fit her perfectly. I found Rhett at a pet adoption center a couple of months after I got Ashley, and it was love at first sight. Although I call him Rhett Butler, he's nothing like his namesake. Unlike Ashley, who's a very independent young lady, Rhett's what you'd call a mama's boy. He's always snuggling and can't seem to get petted enough. Like Ashley, he's smoky gray too, with long, soft fur and gold eyes. If I'm not up in time to suit this pair, Ashley will actually pull the sheets off me. I wonder if they know who's really the boss.

The first thing I do once I'm out of bed is about five minutes of stretching, and then I hit the floor for twenty-five sit-ups. I do these with my knees bent, feet flat on the floor, and my hands clasped behind my head. It's important to breathe correctly (inhale while you're lying flat on your back, exhale on the sitting up part) and not to use your arms to "pull" your head foward. Next, I brush my teeth, make my bed, then do twenty-five more sit-ups, followed by fifteen girl-style push-ups. Although I also do aerobic exercise (jumping rope, running in place on a trampoline, riding a stationary bicycle, or jogging) as often as I can, sometimes all I have time for is this little morning routine. The sit-ups work the abdominals, and the push-ups help increase upper-body strength and tone. I know—from experience, I'm ashamed to say—how easy it is to neglect your body. But I've found that if you stick with a program, it gets to be a habit, and habits—even good ones—are hard to break. Now I feel sluggish and tired if I don't exercise every day.

Downstairs, I put on a pot of freshly ground, cinnamon-spiced coffee, bring in the morning paper, feed the cats, and go through my schedule for the day. I rarely eat breakfast. In fact, I've found that the best way to diet and keep my weight where I want it is to follow no specific regimen at all. I know this sounds too easy to be true, and you're probably thinking, "Well, look at her. She was born with that body." Hardly. I was once twenty-five pounds heavier than I am now and no surprise, either. I rarely had fresh fruits and vegetables, and ate whatever my body craved. That turned out to be a big mistake, because having been raised on southern home cooking and being a confirmed fan of such diet no-nos as chocolate, fast food, and sweets of all descriptions, I ate all wrong. Now, that's not to say I didn't enjoy it, because I did. I just hated the way it made me look and feel. To this day, even as I dutifully spoon up a nutritious hot cereal, bran flakes, or yogurt at breakfast, deep inside there's a voice crying out for Frosted Flakes, Captain Crunch, deep-fried French toast, or chocolate milk.

From experience, I know that the sure way to talk yourself off a diet is to convince yourself that (a) dieting is taking all the fun out of your life, and (b) that you're missing something. Again, the key is to use your common sense. There's no reason why you have to eat three meals a day. If you really think about it, you'll see that many of us eat out of habit. Just because it's "dinnertime" doesn't always mean that you need to eat. Listen to your body. If you aren't that hungry, just have a nutritious snack, maybe a salad, a baked potato (but no sour cream, butter, or other fattening toppings), or some fresh fruit and perhaps a small piece of cheese. Also, think about your day. If you know, for example, that you'll be having a big dinner, eat a lighter lunch (or none at all). Similarly, if you know that you overate the night before, eat lightly the next day. And watch that scale! If I see that I've put on a pound or two, I cut way back until that weight's gone. It only takes a few days, and I haven't put on enough weight to be depressed about it (there's another obstacle to dieting!). It all comes down to keeping it under control. Not only do you look better, but just knowing that you're in charge of your body (and not vice versa) can really brighten your general attitude and boost your self-confidence.

Of course, I still crave those "forbidden" foods, and I still eat them now and then. I just think about them differently. You know that when you really want something that's either fattening or not real nutritious, or both, what you really want most is just to taste it, right? So, if I decide that I really want Kentucky Fried Chicken, I'll buy one piece. Where I'd once down a whole package of cookies, I'll eat a 120-calorie granola bar, or turn what used to be a daily ritual (lunch at Wendy's, White Castle, or McDonald's) into an occasional treat.

If you feel that you absolutely must indulge yourself, do it away from home. And don't waste your big ice-cream experience on anything less than the best—the flavor that you really, really want, the brand that you love. If you crave a piece of cake, get something truly scrumptious from a great restaurant or bakery, not something you just microwaved and frosted in fifteen minutes. Even if it's fast food that you're dying for, go and get it—and never bring any extra home. No matter how much you tell yourself that you're only going to eat one cookie, the other fifty in your cabinet will somehow lure you back. And face it, nobody ever throws these things out in the trash. The only way they ever leave the premises is on you.

Thankfully, once you get used to looking and feeling better, those cravings slowly diminish. Until they do, though, you have to deal with these as reasonably as you can. I figure that if an occasional dish of Häagen-Dazs cookies-and-cream or a monthly serving of onion rings will make it easier for me to stick to my good eating habits the other ninety-five percent of the time, it's a small sacrifice. Often, dieters "do without" for so long, then go off and binge, and we all know what happens then.

In the long run, it's also fortunate that I'm not much of a cook. My mother made great lasagne and chili, and I have a couple of favorite dishes that I prepare on those rare occasions when I cook for a small dinner party. Then I'll make some southern specialty, like chicken and dumplings. Most of the time, though, especially when I'm preparing something for myself, I keep it simple: salads, tuna in water, egg salad, broiled chicken (no fats, grease, or chicken skin), and steamed or raw vegetables.

But back to my typical day. Before I do anything else, I review my day's schedule. I'm basically a very organized person—I make lists of things to do, and I like everything to be neat and in its place. It's annoying to have to waste precious time doing something as mundane as looking for your keys or trying to remember something you weren't supposed to forget.

If it happens to be one of the two days a week that we're taping *Wheel of Fortune,* I follow pretty much the same routine. After breakfast, I shower and wash my hair, which I let dry naturally, take my vitamins, don my standard everyday clothes (usually jeans or sweats and sneakers), and take care of miscellaneous errands, like food shopping, meeting with my manager, and banking. At around a quarter to one, I leave for the studios at Burbank, about a ten-minute drive from my house.

Most days I enter the studio building with my arms full. I have a few samples from my renowned collection of cheap (I mean under fifteen dollars a pair) shoes that I bring just in case I need something to match an outfit, my latest afghan project, and several pieces of fan mail. I really enjoy reading and replying to my mail. I remember how crushed I was when, several years before, John Travolta didn't respond to my fan letter. I vowed then that if I ever became famous enough for people to write to me, I'd answer as many letters as I could.

One of the best parts of my job is hearing from my fans. I get everything from marriage proposals to invitations to watermelon festivals. People send me magazine covers to autograph, and lots and lots of questions. I try to answer as many letters that ask for an answer as I can. Of course, I can't answer every single one, but here are some tips for when you write. First, try to keep your letter brief and to the point. The more direct the questions, the better I can answer them. Second, write on the outside of your envelope what you're writing for—a picture, an autograph, a reply, whatever. That really helps to speed things up. And third, write legibly so that my reply goes to the correct address.

My first stop is my dressing room. Although it's mine only when we're taping, it's still my home away from home. It's furnished with a couch, vanity and chair, television, a few small tables, and has a private bathroom. And, of course, there are my clothes. I suppose that next to turning the letters, I'm most famous for the clothes I wear on the show. At least that's the only conclusion I can draw from the questions I'm asked. Of the ten most popular questions, eight concern my clothes (the other two—about the puzzle board—are answered later on). Here they are:

1. What size do you wear?

A perfect size 5, which is handy, since I don't have to try on every single outfit beforehand. Most times, everything fits or needs only very minor alterations.

2. Do you get to keep the clothes you wear?

No. They're all lent to the show in exchange for the little promotional blurb you see at the end of the credits. I wear some of the clothes when I do promotional appearances or go out of town on contestant searches for the show. After I wear them, they're either returned to the store or designer, or they are auctioned off with the proceeds going to charity.

3. Who makes the clothes?

As of now, my outfits all come from Gucci, Giorgio of Beverly Hills, New Leaf, Climax, Gitano, or Pacino.

4. Do you get to pick the clothes you wear?

No, I don't. Usually, the designers send samples of their latest designs. It's been our experience that there's a certain number of people in the audience who love to see me in any given style. We try to keep it interesting by using a wide range of looks and styles. As you probably know if you watch *Wheel of Fortune,* each show has its own look. For the daytime show, I'm usually wearing more casual sportswear in perky "up" colors, like peaches, greens, pinks, and other pastels. For the syndicated nighttime version, it's strictly the glamour look, in beaded gowns, some actually pretty daring, in a wide range of lengths and styles.

5. Do you like every single outfit you wear on the show?

To be perfectly honest about it, not every piece is something that I would wear offstage. Of course, my own personal taste in clothes is very eclectic —I can feel comfortable wearing a soft silk blouse and tailored pants one day, then going out in a white miniskirt and boots the next. Basically, though, I have always been a clotheshorse, so trying on lots of different things (which I'd encourage everybody to do anyway)—whether I like each thing or not—has its own rewards. Sometimes I'll find that I look better than I expected I would in something I'd never picture myself wearing.

6. *Are the clothes expensive?*

No. Surprisingly, most items retail for between $60 and $150 dollars each. Of course, there are exceptions, but generally most things aren't as expensive as they look.

7. *Where can the clothes be bought?*

Most major department and women's stores carry these lines. Just the other day, I was walking down the street and saw a store window full of mannequins, and each was wearing a dress I'd worn on the show. You can also write to the designers for the address of the store nearest you that carries their line.

8. *Do you ever wear the same item more than once?*

Occasionally, but more often on the daytime show than on the nighttime version.

I know wearing clothes sounds like a pretty simple task, but there's more to it than that. I couldn't get along without my wardrobe mistress, Florence Calce. She has been with NBC for over twenty years and has worked as a costume maker for Dean Martin,

Flip Wilson, *Laugh-In*, a couple of soap operas, and many other shows. Her job is to see to it that everything is in order and to make any minor alterations, which she can do in a flash.

About once a month Florence will meet me at my house and we'll go to Beverly Hills, where I try on clothes. Usually our producer, Nancy Jones, will have phoned either Gucci or Giorgio ahead of time so that when Florence and I arrive, there's a rack of gorgeous things in my size just waiting to be tried on. In under two hours, I'll have tried on dozens of things, of which Florence and I will finally select only fourteen or so. Now, this is my idea of fun.

Once in my dressing room, Florence and I will go over which outfits I'll be wearing, then we'll pick out shoes and accessories for each. I also keep handy a big plastic compartmentalized box of inexpensive (one to five dollars a piece) costume jewelry—made out of anything from plastic to rhinestones. I think that you can never have too many accessories. After all, a good wardrobe isn't a lot of clothes, it's a lot of looks.

My next stop is my hairstylist, a woman named D.J. Plumb. She knows what clothes I'll be wearing and in what order, so she's already formulated some ideas about each of the five hairstyles. First thing she does is put in a bunch of hot rollers, which stay in while I'm having my makeup done.

Being a former model, I know a lot about makeup, but I'd never attempt to do my own for television.

The lighting is so "unnatural" that you really need an expert, and I've got one of the best, Bruce Grayson. The son of another famous makeup specialist, Dave Grayson, Bruce is a perfectionist. On the average, I spend between forty-five minutes and an hour in makeup. By the time Bruce has finished patting, sponging, blending, and highlighting, I feel totally transformed. Then it's into my first outfit for the day (usually the tightest; Florence knows me well enough to save the looser things for after our dinner break) and then back to D.J., who combs out my hair and shapes it into whatever style will complement what I'm wearing.

Every once in a while we'll make what seems to be a minor change, and after that show airs, I'll be deluged with mail. A certain dress can prompt compliments and complaints. But I think that the main subject of my mail has been my hair. Over the years I've gone from semistraight, longish, light-brown hair to a shorter, layered, frosted blond look. My stylist, Joseph Genna of the Allen Edwards Salon in Beverly Hills, did his best to make each small change as gradually as possible, but it wasn't gradual enough. Once we got a ton of mail when my hair came out just a touch blonder than usual.

If, after all this, I've got a few spare minutes, I'll crochet a few rows on my latest project. Ever since 1983, when Kim Salvatore, an earlier hairdresser on the show, taught me how to crochet, it's become my favorite hobby. Not only is crocheting relaxing and totally portable (I've made a lot of progress by carrying my crocheting with me on plane flights), but sooner or later you have something to show for your efforts. Although I'm not really an expert, I've perfected one stitch, which I use in the following afghan pattern.

AFGHAN INSTRUCTIONS

Size: Instructions are for full-size afghan—approximately 49″ by 58″.
(Baby blanket—approximately 24″ by 28″.)
Materials: Knitting worsted-weight yarn in your favorite color (3.5 oz. skeins)—about 14(4) skeins.
Size G crochet hook or size needed to crochet to gauge.
Gauge: 5 dc = 1″; 4 rows = 1¾″.

Note 1: Afghan and baby blanket are both made in one piece.
Note 2: The afghan is made in a tight gauge for maximum density and warmth. If you like a looser gauge, use a larger hook and expect to use a little more yarn.

AFGHAN—Loosely ch 291(141). **Row 1:** Starting in fourth ch from hook (turning ch-3 counts as 1 dc), work 1 dc in each ch across—289(139) dc. Ch 2, turn (counts as first dc of next row). **Row 2:** Skip first dc, working through back loops only, work 1 dc in each dc across. Ch 2, turn. Repeat Row 2 10(2) times more—12(4) rows of dc in all. On last row of dc, ch 5 to turn.

MESH: Row 1: Skip first 3 dc, 1 dc in next dc, * ch 2, skip 2 dc, 1 dc in next dc, repeat from * across, working last dc in turning ch. Ch 2, turn. **Row 2:** Skip first dc, working through back loops only, * work 1 dc in each of next 2 ch, a dc in next dc, repeat from * across. Ch 5, turn. Repeat Rows 1 and 2 once more, followed by one more repeat of Row 1. Now, work 12(4) rows of dc, again working through back loops only. Continue to alternate mesh pattern with 12(4) rows of dc, until you have 6 sets of mesh and 7 sets of 12(4)-row dc. Fasten off.

If it's about three in the afternoon, it's time to start taping the first of the five shows we'll do that day. After we've completed either two or three shows, we'll break for dinner. Once as I entered the dining room, one of the caterers said, "Here comes the eating machine," and on several occasions I've overheard contestants muse aloud about how I could eat so much and still stay so thin. I usually sit with Bruce, Florence, D.J., Pat Sajak, and a few other people. Altogether, about sixty people work on the show, and during breaks we just sit around and talk about the latest gossip, good movies we've seen, or what we did last weekend. It's basically the usual office chat.

After an hour or so, it's back to work, which for me means my third or fourth outfit and hairstyle change of the day. We do the remainder of the shows for a new audience, and if all goes well, the day ends around eight that night. I gather up my things, sign a few autographs, say good-bye to everyone, and drive home. On the rare evening that I'm not too tired, I may meet some friends for drinks or take in a movie. Usually, though, I walk in my front door, kick off my shoes, cuddle and feed Rhett and Ashley, and just relax. I might catch the late news, then watch the *Tonight* show and *Late Night with David Letterman*, make a few calls or read a good nonfiction book (any autobiography) or my favorite magazine, *Architectural Digest*, before I fall asleep.

No matter what my day brings, I can count on having less time to take care of personal things than I'd like. Having worked as a professional model since 1976, I've picked up lots of beauty, makeup, and fashion tips that save time and money. Additionally, I've amassed a number of what you'd call household hints that also minimize the time and effort I have to expend on those things.

Around the house I try to get the most work done with the least effort. That means washing all my clothes (except things I want to shrink) in cold water, using vinegar on the bathroom chrome to remove soap scum without scrubbing, and removing the occasional pet odor from the carpet with a raw onion or ammonia. You can also find a wealth of uses for the most common household products. I clean jewelry with regular toothpaste. You can use a toothbrush, but I prefer just rubbing in the toothpaste with my fingers. This works especially well on even the most tarnished sterling silver. Watering your houseplants with the water you've hard-boiled eggs in gives them extra nutrients, especially calcium.

I rarely have the time to undertake major reorganization projects, so I try to do a little bit every day. For example, in the closet I've always kept a box where I'll toss anything—old towels, household items—that I no longer want. Every so often I'll have a yard sale or give the stuff away.

One exception to this rule is clothes, which I usually keep forever. First, a style will come back sooner or later. Second, there's a lot you can do to update and "recycle" certain items, particularly sweaters and shirts. Big sweaters, blue jeans, and accessories almost never go out of style. Besides, even if you think you don't have the right outfit for a certain pair of earrings or shoes, keep them anyway. Who knows what you'll have next year, or even next week? And you know these things—no matter how cheap they are—only get more expensive over time. When a sweater or shirt does seem to have outlived its usefulness, try adding shoulder pads, beads, and other details.

Using your wardrobe and accessories to create a whole look is really the key. People rarely recall a particular detail as often as they recall your whole look. For that reason, it's crucial that you always dress before a full-length mirror. You'll be amazed how changing just one detail—like the shoes you're wearing—can really change the whole look.

But, you're probably saying, I don't look good in this or that, it's just not me. How do you know until you've tried it? A department store dressing room is not the place to try new looks, your bedroom mirror is. There's no law that says you have to be faithful to one particular style. If you must dress conservatively for your job, there's no reason why you can't dress a little more playfully outside the office, and even the smallest details can add to the transition. Mousse up your hair a little, wear a shorter skirt, try some outrageous costume jewelry. Just try it.

Again, accessories are the key. It's a lot less expensive—and a lot more fun—to buy one great black dress and several sets of accessories—belts, shoes, bags, costume jewelry, hats, stockings, scarves—in a range of styles and colors. Plus you can use those accessories to expand other outfits. Once you get started, the possibilities will increase tenfold with every new piece you buy. I learned this back when I first came to Hollywood and needed an instant wardrobe with a wide range of looks for auditions and interviews. Even though I can now better afford to buy more things, I still enjoy seeing how much I can achieve just by being resourceful and using my imagination.

The great thing about clothes is that when worn properly, they can enhance your best features and draw attention away from those you're not so happy about. The way you wear your clothes and what you wear can make a difference in how you look by about ten pounds either way. The secret to achieving these "illusions" is a sense of proportion.

Everyone's body is different. Be honest with yourself, and don't get hung up on liking an article just because it's your favorite color or your best friend looks great in the same style. How does it look on you? Does it make your figure look slim, and does it accentuate your best features or not? A small-hipped, large-breasted woman should try and balance her appearance by wearing clothes that accentuate her hips, while someone with the opposite figure type— small-breasted but with a large derriere or hips— should wear loose-fitting or blouson tops. A wide belt at the waist cuts you in half, where a belt worn a little more loosely just over the hips will draw attention to your hips.

Colors, patterns, and textures of fabrics will also add or detract from the look you want to achieve. No matter how you wear it, black lace will always have a sexy connotation, while a gray wool skirt will probably always look like it belongs in the office, no matter what you do with it. Vertical stripes or lines will create an illusion of tallness, while horizontal stripes or designs make you look shorter and wider.

The first step to beauty is good health and fitness, which means good food, exercise, and plenty of sleep. My basic beauty philosophy is to do a little something for yourself every single day. Again, this means getting into good habits, like pushing back all your cuticles (fingers and toes) in the shower each morning, doing minor eyebrow tweezing every day, and briskly scrubbing your whole body with a Buf-Puf or loofah sponge.

My skin varies from dry to slightly oily. When it feels oily, I wash my face with soap and water. At other times, I use a gentle cleansing cream, then put on a general moisturizer, being careful to put extra Vitamin E oil under my eyes and on my neck. I also use moisturizer under my foundation, which is usually a water-base liquid makeup. Before I go to sleep each night, I'm careful to remove every trace of makeup with a cleansing cream, using soft cotton balls or a clean cotton washcloth.

I know that much of what you read about me in the press suggests that I made it on my looks alone and that clothes are what matter most to me. That couldn't be further from the truth. I believe that success—in anything—depends on who, not what, you are. More than that, it involves hard work and having a dream.

2

♥

Whenever I think about my life and how I grew up, or whenever something important happens—whether it's happy or sad—I think of my mother, Joan Marie Nicholas White. As soon as you mention that you're from a small, southern, tourist beach town, most people assume that your life was boring or that your folks were typical, small-town people. But while it's true that my childhood was pretty normal, it was anything but boring, thanks to my mother, who was the most interesting and inspiring person I've ever known.

Momma was born on June 2, 1936, to an unwed woman of Italian-German heritage in Syracuse, New

York. This woman's family forbade her to marry Momma's father because they felt that he was socially beneath her. Though many years later Momma did learn more about her natural mother and even once confronted her natural father, she never discussed what she'd learned about her natural parents, at least not with me. As far as Momma was concerned, her parents were the couple who adopted her, Luther Romain Nicholas and his wife, Alta Albertine Trumble Nicholas, a distant relative of my maternal grandmother.

The Nicholases were living in Constantia, New York, near Lake Oneida, and were both in their early fifties when they learned that a baby was due. They could never have a child and so desperately wanted one that they not only agreed to adopt the baby despite their advancing age, but did so informally. Because the adoption was not handled through the courts and was not technically legal, my grandparents took Momma from the hospital when she was just a few days old, and immediately left the town where they'd lived all their lives to move south.

They set out with no definite destination, but they settled in Ocean Drive Beach, South Carolina, a very small town, which was later consolidated with several other little towns into what is now North Myrtle Beach, just a few miles south of the North Carolina border. Because of its warm year-round climate and beautiful white-sand beaches, Ocean Drive Beach soon became popular with tourists. Granddaddy was a carpenter, and Grandma stayed home to care for the baby Joan Marie.

Momma grew up in a modest wood-frame house located at the corner of Route 17 and Main Street. My grandparents lived there until it was torn down in 1970 or so to make way for an amusement park. From the outside, it wouldn't strike you as the nicest house in town—I remember it looking sort of run-down, unpainted, with a front porch that always sagged. There was no running water, central heating, or indoor plumbing. Water had to be hand pumped from a well and carried into the house, and even when I was little, they still used an outhouse. But my grandparents, who owned other property in the area and back in New York state, never seemed to mind it, and neither did I. No doubt they could afford something better, but it was enough for them.

I have wonderful memories of sitting on that old porch in a rocking chair with my grandfather and feeding squirrels and blue jays out of my hand. Grandmama made the inside very homey, with large, overstuffed chairs and little scatter rugs. There was also a very large strawberry patch on the property, which my grandfather tended, and he sold the berries for extra money. From the start, I was an enthusiastic picker myself, but it was clear that I wasn't destined to make my living at it, since I favored my own pick-one, eat-one harvesting method.

My mother was always a very good child, who rarely asked her parents for anything. What my grandparents couldn't give her in material things they more than made up for by lavishing attention on her.

Even as a very young kid, Momma was precocious and spirited. One of her dearest friends told me a story about Momma that describes her perfectly. In the forties, when Momma was just eleven, some local high school kids approached her and asked her to go into a store and get them some beer. Despite her youth, my mother had "connections," and though the older kids were afraid to try to buy it themselves, my mother gamely agreed to do it—for a fee. She went into the store and returned a few minutes later with a big paper sack full of beer, which she turned over only *after* she'd been paid.

Throughout her life, Momma would be known to everyone in North Myrtle Beach for her spunkiness, and she was something of a local legend all her life because of it. Whatever Momma wanted, she just went after it. She never seemed to be afraid of anything.

Around the time Momma was twelve, she learned that she was an adopted child. My grandparents told her the truth after they'd learned that Momma's natural mother had died of cancer at age forty. Soon after, they went to court and completed the legal adoption process. According to some folks, completing this formality meant that my grandparents could finally relax, free of the fear that someone might take their child away.

Sometime after Momma learned this, she went to

Syracuse to visit some relatives and discovered where her natural father worked. He owned a bar, and Momma went in, ordered a drink, and just watched him for a while. Finally she approached him and told him that she was his daughter. He said, "I don't have a daughter." At that, Momma pushed his face toward a mirror and said, "Look! That mirror doesn't lie." Apparently they looked very much alike. I think that was the first and the last time she ever saw him.

My grandparents were very proud of my mother. She was smart and beautiful. In a photograph taken when she was nineteen, Momma has a sweet, demure little smile that belies her adventurous—and I guess you might say, a little bit wild—nature. Her black hair and brown eyes gave her an attractive, slightly Mediterranean look that I'm sure seemed quite exotic in that little town. Though she stood just a little over five foot two, she had a commanding presence.

She was very outgoing and always popular and, like me, a good student who never studied. She was a cheerleader at Wampee High School, and it was around this time that she got her reputation as a great dancer with beautiful legs, of which she was very proud.

When Momma graduated high school in 1953, her parents were well into their sixties. Still, there was nothing too good for her. They gave her a brand-new Pontiac to drive to the University of South Carolina, where she stayed for only about a semester before returning home. Back in North Myrtle Beach she went to work as a waitress at a drive-in restaurant owned by the parents of actor Christopher George. She and Christopher became lifelong friends.

Momma had her share of interesting experiences, though no one could pull anything over on her, even at that young age. She worked as a carhop, and once she brought an order to a man, only to discover that he was exposing himself to her. Without a second's thought, she gave him exactly what she thought he deserved—a naked lap full of scalding hot coffee.

At some point Momma met and fell very deeply in love with a young man named Nicky. On May 28, 1953, just two weeks before she and Nicky were to wed, he was killed in a car accident. Momma never told me much more than that about him. Not long after his death, she left her hometown and moved to Miami, where, within a few months, she met my father, Miguel Angel Rosich, or Mike, as he was called. Mike's father was German and his mother was Spanish; he was born in Puerto Rico. He'd recently moved to Miami, where he worked as an elevator operator. He was extremely handsome in the classic Latin sense, very dark, with brown eyes and a finely chiseled, very angular face. Looking at his old pictures, I think that he could have been a model; he was that good-looking.

My mother fell madly in love with him not long after they met. She and he were eating alone at separate tables in a Miami café. When she got up to leave, he paid her check, and they started talking. Even though he was about seven years older and from a totally different background, they married and moved back to Momma's hometown.

When my grandparents met Mike, they were less than thrilled, though I've never really understood just why. Basically, I think that my grandparents were very small-town people who'd never really known anyone from a background as different from their own as my father's. Maybe they thought that Momma was too young or still on the rebound from Nicky's death, or maybe Mike was just too different. Maybe they worried that he couldn't support my mother, working as he did then as a garage mechanic. Who knows? Whatever their objections, they didn't stop my mother from marrying him in early 1956.

Shortly after their marriage my parents moved to New York City, and that spring Momma found out that she was expecting. For some reason Momma wasn't crazy about New York. Having moved from the comfort of a small town to a big city, I can understand how she might have felt overwhelmed, especially with her first baby on the way. By the end of the year, my parents had moved back to North Myrtle Beach and taken an apartment over the Pad, a now-legendary beach hangout where the cool crowd drank and did the shag, the southern version of the jitterbug Momma was so good at.

It was my father's twenty-eighth birthday—and Momma was just barely twenty-one—when I was born on Monday, February 18, 1957, at 2:35 P.M. There was no maternity hospital along the Grand Strand, the sixty-mile strip of beach that includes North Myrtle Beach, so I was born at the Conway Hospital, in Conway, South Carolina, about a half hour's drive away.

Weighing in at six pounds, nine ounces, with blue eyes (which later turned brown) and brown hair, I was probably much like every other baby—though reading through my baby book, you'd think I was the greatest baby ever born. My father filled in all the blanks with details about me, all written in a fine, beautifully formed art deco–style script. My first "press" read: "Head round as a ball, turned up nose. Eighteen inches long with a twelve-inch chest."

They named me Vanna Marie Rosich. The "Marie" was after my mother's middle name, and "Vanna" was after my grandmother's godchild, Vana Worrell, the granddaughter of Momma's next-door neighbors, the A. A. Worrells. Momma added the second *n* just to make it different.

Judging from the black and white snapshots and the loving entries in my baby book, ours was a normal, happy young family. But things were far from perfect. Though friends and relatives have since offered their theories as to why my parents broke up, all I know is what Momma told me: She and my father just couldn't live together. One major disagreement they had was over where to live. He wanted to go back to New York City, and Momma refused to go. Before my first birthday, my father left and moved back to New York, and Momma and I moved in with my grandparents.

Because Momma had to work to support us, she went back to Miami and I stayed with my grandparents, who basically raised me and spoiled me rotten. I was a normal baby, walking and talking on schedule. By April 1958 my vocabulary consisted of "Momma," "puppy," "kitty," "car," "oh-oh," "see," "more," and—what else?—"bye-bye." Later that year Momma met the man who I would always think of as my daddy, Herbert Stackley White, Jr.

Daddy was born on September 6, 1926, in Lake City, South Carolina. Because his father, Herbert White, Sr., had trouble finding work during the Great Depression, his family moved around often, finally settling in Dillon, South Carolina, in the late thirties. He lived there with his parents and six siblings until he joined the army, serving two years in Korea. After he came home, he traveled with a friend to Arizona, and there he went to work for the post office.

Daddy had always loved the beach, so he returned to South Carolina and opened a snack bar in North Myrtle Beach. He was looking for help, and Momma was looking for a job, and that's how they met. Though he was about ten years older than Momma, they hit it off right away. In terms of looks, he was the total opposite of my father. He had brown hair and blue eyes, and he was very handsome, but in a different way. She asked him to dance at the Pad, and he later told me that when they got up to dance, everyone in the place cleared the floor and watched. About a year later, on October 11, 1959, she and Daddy were married in a quiet church ceremony.

Of course I was too young to know what was going on. I remember that my mother was all dressed up in a very nice, conservative suit and that I was all dolled up for the occasion. I think the meaning of it all finally hit me when we moved from my grand-parents' house and into our own—and I discovered that I had to listen to and mind Daddy. I don't think anyone had been as firm with me as he was, and it was a rude awakening. I didn't remember my natural father, so it wasn't a question of resenting Daddy; it was just that, like Momma, I had a mind of my own and didn't like being told what to do.

One day at Grandmama's I'd pulled out every pot and pan and was making quite a racket. She pleaded with me to stop, but I just kept it up. Exasperated, she called Daddy on the phone and told him what was happening. He walked in, picked me up, gave me a whack (which I'm sure I deserved), and that was that. No doubt this was the surprise of my young life. But I got the message.

Our first house (we lived in three while I was grow-ing up, all within two blocks of one another) was just a few hundred feet behind the drive-in restaurant my parents ran. I'd go to the restaurant to get a hamburger or hot dog and shake. I remember Momma working the counter and Daddy minding the grill. Because North Myrtle Beach's economy depended on the tourist trade, business usually fell off during the winter, so when Momma discovered that she was pregnant in early 1960, she and Daddy decided that it would be better for Momma to be at home instead of at the drive-in.

I loved having Momma home with me all day. She was always talking to me and telling me things. Then just a month before my parents' first wedding anniversary, on September 3, 1960, my brother Herbert Stackley White III was born—like me at 2:35, but A.M., not P.M. From the beginning, we called him Chip, as in chip off the old block, and from the first day I saw him, I loved him. At three and a half I wasn't really a baby myself anymore and could begin to grasp the idea of being his big sister, a role I loved. I'd stand by his playpen or crib and just watch him sleep for hours. People tell me I was very protective of Chip, even as a little girl. I still am today, even though he towers over me and protects me sometimes too.

Shortly after his birth, Momma decided that she wanted to go into business for herself. Many women would think that two little kids would be more than enough to keep them busy, but not Momma. She had more energy than anyone I've ever seen. There was simply no stopping her. I always picture her, cigarette in hand, cup of instant coffee in front of her, doing something—always doing something. She got bored easily, and doing things like running a house or cooking weren't fulfilling enough. Fortunately, Daddy not only understood Momma, he encouraged her.

I sometimes think that she was born thirty years before her time. She had the brains and the drive to have done anything she wanted. In different times maybe she would have become a professional of some sort. As it was, though, she had to settle for running the office-supply business she and Daddy started on a couple thousand dollars they'd saved from the restaurant. They christened their new venture J&H, for Joan and Herbert.

Since Daddy had taken a full-time job at the post office, Momma did everything—typing, bookkeeping, selling, handling the taxes. She was only twenty-four, but once she set her mind to it, she would learn how to do whatever she wanted, usually by doing it. Momma was always willing to help anyone who needed it too. I can't count the number of friends and relatives who lived with us at one time or another, either because they'd had a financial setback or some major crisis in their lives. Momma would move them in, feed them, help them any way she could.

As soon as Momma went back to work, we got our first maid, Hattie Mae Wilson, a black woman who cooked, looked after Chip and me, and ran the house. Chip and I were normal kids who enjoyed doing typical things. We'd play games like Simon Says and Hide and Seek. Chip had a tree house, and I had a playhouse with a kitchen where I would prepare meals, like tree-bark entrées with leaf-and-grass vegetables. My favorite toy, though, was my Barbie doll, for whom I had a dream house and tons of clothes. And I loved my toy vanity, play makeup, a mink stole, and little high heels, which made me feel very glamorous and quite grown-up.

In the first years the office-supply business flourished, and so my parents bought an even larger space in a building with a second-floor apartment that provided additional income. With Momma and Daddy working so hard, we settled into a routine. The post office where Daddy worked closed around five o'clock, and Momma would close shop so they'd both get home in time for dinner at six. We always ate at the same time, and dinner was family time, which Chip and I looked forward to.

After Hattie Mae left to work for a neighbor, we found Carrie, a woman who lived across the street from my grandparents, to take over for us. Carrie was a large, warm, loving woman in her thirties. She was also a great cook. You couldn't beat her southern dishes; she made the best fried chicken, string beans, and fresh banana pudding. When I think of Carrie, I picture her sitting in the living room, ironing and watching her soap operas on television. If she caught me doing anything bad, she'd make me sit quietly in a little chair with my hands folded in my lap. And despite Daddy's and Momma's considerable efforts, I still had a stubborn streak (still do). Carrie would threaten to tell my parents if I'd been bad, but more often than not, my misbehavior went unreported. I really loved Carrie and came to think of her as family.

Of course, nobody's childhood is perfect, but mine was probably about as good as it gets. Not only did I have loving parents and an adorable little brother, but I lived in a wonderful little town where it seemed—at least to a little girl—that nobody had a care in the world. Though hundreds of thousands of people passed through the town during the tourist season, the permanent population never exceeded a few thousand. I always describe it as the kind of place where you could lie down in the middle of Main Street for three hours and never worry about getting hit. (Of course, this was true only during the off season.) Times change, even in North Myrtle Beach, but back then we never even locked our front doors at night or took the keys out of the car when we parked it. Crime was something you only heard about happening someplace else. All of the parents had grown up together, and all of their kids would grow up together. It might sound like a corny thing to say, but my childhood was like something Norman Rockwell might have painted. I still feel that I was very lucky to grow up as I did.

As I got older, I became fascinated by the idea of going to school. Other kids on the block were going, and it struck me that school would be great. I couldn't wait. When I finally entered first grade at Ocean Drive Elementary in the fall of 1963, I was not disappointed. Momma had gotten me new clothes for school, and I loved every single day—in fact, most years I had perfect attendance, something noted on many of my report cards.

Every day was something new, and I got excellent grades. Of course, that doesn't mean I was a model student. My early enthusiasm for front-row desks waned when I found out that you could do more talking during class if you sat at the back. And even that didn't always help. My first-grade teacher wrote in a report card: "Good worker, but she is often out of her seat and talking to others!" I can't count how many hundreds of times I wrote "I will not talk in class" during my school career. I do know it was enough that I went to the trouble of devising time- and labor-saving efforts to do it more quickly, like writing a column of "I"s, then a column of "will"s, and so on, until I'd served my sentence, so to speak.

It was during my first school years that I developed two lifelong loves—boys and friendly competition. From the very start, I was absolutely boy crazy. I just loved them! Even though I was generally an out-going kid, I was shy around boys, but that didn't stop me from having "boyfriends" from the first grade on. I was also becoming a keen competitor. My game? Marbles! I wanted to be the very best marble shooter, so each day before school I'd go through my big sock of marbles to pick out the marbles I'd take to school and "gamble" with that day. Even then I was prag- matic about it. I'd put aside all my favorites, then estimate just how many of the rest I could stand to lose, usually about ten or fifteen, and these were all I'd take.

Like all kids, Chip and I loved the holidays, especially Christmas. I suppose that our Christmas celebrations were much like everyone else's; still, those memories have stayed with me. In fact, while we're trimming the tree in my home, I still play the same Johnny Mathis Christmas album that my parents played when I was a kid.

I remember helping Momma unwrap the ornaments, some of which were quite old and fragile. Every day Chip and I would come home from school to find more presents under the tree, and with Momma and Daddy gone all day at work, we could have sneaked lots of peeks, but we never did. We saved up our dollar-a-week allowances—earned by doing chores, keeping our rooms clean, and getting good grades—and bought Momma a blouse or nightgown and Daddy some after-shave or handkerchiefs.

Every Christmas Eve we watched *Rudolph the Red-Nosed Reindeer* (which I still watch), and Chip and I each got to open one gift. Then off to bed, where I'd lie awake, looking out the window for Santa's arrival and listening to hear him eating the cookies we'd left out for him. The next morning we'd descend upon the gifts, never wondering why Santa's thank-you note was in Daddy's handwriting or figuring out just how Santa got in. It was always a wonderful day, and we were never disappointed. It was also during Christmas and Thanksgiving that we'd all drive over to Dillon, South Carolina, to visit Daddy's parents, Herbert and Marie White, whom we referred to as Grandma and Grandaddy White, and his sister, my dear Aunt Virginia.

Not only was Christmas my favorite holiday, it also provided the opportunity for my stage debut. I sang "It's Beginning to Look a Lot Like Christmas" for my first-grade play, all decked out in a poinsettia costume—a green jumpsuit with a red "floral" headpiece. The following year I played a snowflake, and my career really began to take off the following Easter when I reigned as the queen of Ocean Drive Elementary during the Easter parade program and later won a Miss Hollywood little girls' beauty pageant.

As I got older, I loved school all the more. One of my favorite—and best—subjects was spelling. I had a photographic memory, so I didn't have to study that hard to get good grades.

In third grade I joined the Brownies and started taking piano lessons, which my grandparents paid for with money they earned selling strawberries. My grandmother had always hoped that I would eventually play piano in church.

I also grew to love things that most little girls think are kind of yucky, like crawling around in dusty underground forts full of spiders and snakes, "spying" on people from under the house, and playing with lizards. One of my favorite things to do was to put a little string leash around a chameleon's leg, tie the other end to a safety pin, and pin the lizard to me and watch it change to the color of my outfit. At one point, my best friend, Beth Johnson, and I had "adopted" an alligator who lived in a pond near my grandparents' next-door neighbor, Mr. Worrell. The 'gator's name was Mr. Bill, and we fed him pieces of raw meat from the end of a barbecue fork. Oblivious of the danger, we got pretty close to Mr. Bill and never thought much about it, until one day when Chip fell asleep in a parked car and my parents went crazy, thinking Mr. Bill had eaten him. Boy, was I relieved when Chip finally turned up—in one piece. Also, I'd spent lots of time fishing in that pond. Basically, I was a brave little kid, but I still wouldn't bait my own hooks when we went fishing. (In fact, I still won't.)

I was about nine or ten years old when I decided that I wanted to be on TV. I'd always loved watching my favorite shows, such as *I Love Lucy*, *Bewitched*, *Bonanza*, and *Dr. Kildare*, but I especially liked *Rat Patrol* because my "uncle," Christopher George, was on it, playing Sergeant Sam Troy, the leader of a team of World War II commandos. Chip and I never missed a show. I liked to dress up and pretend I was a star of some kind, but when I'd tell my friends that I was going to be a star or be on TV someday, they'd just laugh. I suppose it did sound sort of farfetched back then.

Though my parents' office-supply business had started off strong, business eventually fell off to the point that they decided it wasn't worth working at it any longer. They leased out the building in the late sixties, and Momma went to work selling ads for her friend Polly Lowman's local newspaper. From 1964 through 1968, Momma served on the city council. She also did volunteer work for the Heart Fund, often raising large sums of money.

Carrie was still with us, and I'd grown very close to her. One day in spring, Momma was driving Carrie home for the weekend, and I went along for the ride. Carrie seemed unusually quiet, except to say that she didn't feel so well, until we got to her house. As she got out of the car, she said, "I feel so tired. I feel like walking into the ocean and just keep on walkin' and walkin'."

I remember thinking that this was a very strange thing to say. I had no idea what she meant, but something about the way she said it and the image of walking into the ocean stuck with me. The whole thing seemed sort of scary, though I couldn't put my finger on exactly why. The next day, on Easter, Carrie died. Hers was the first death of anyone close to me, and I took it very hard. Soon after, Eula, a younger woman and a relative of Hattie Mae's, came to work for us. I liked Eula, but I couldn't stop thinking about Carrie. Our family attended the local Methodist church across the street from our house almost every Sunday, so I guess I believed that Carrie had gone to heaven. Still, I couldn't stop thinking about what she'd said. How had she known that she was going to die?

I was all wrapped up in graduating elementary school and making the big step up to junior high, but before the summer was over, my grandmother died. My grandfather followed less than a year after. Both of my grandparents lived with us after their house was torn down. Grandma was very ill by this time and Momma was so devoted to her. I remember seeing Momma brush Grandmama's long, fine blond hair and put it up in a bun. My grandmother died of complications from high blood pressure. My grandfather died, I believe, of a broken heart. He'd loved my grandmother so, he just couldn't go on without her. I was deeply saddened by their passings, and I missed them a great deal, especially my grandmother. I was her pride and joy, and I loved her so dearly. But taking my cue from Momma, I knew that when bad things happen, you must pick yourself up and keep going.

3

♥

As I got older I came to appreciate my parents all the more. Momma especially had a way of teaching me about life. There was no question I could ask that she wouldn't answer truthfully. Momma taught me to be realistic and pragmatic, to always weigh all sides of an issue before making a decision. My mother had been around when she was young, and she and my father both knew that things and people weren't always what they seemed. My parents consistently made a real effort to instill in us good values. Though discipline and hard work were rewarded, we never felt pressured. And most important, they always encouraged us to go after our dreams, no matter how impossible they seemed.

In the fall of 1969 I entered seventh grade. Because Momma believed that Myrtle Beach Junior High was a better school than the one in our district, I transferred there, while all the friends I'd grown up with through elementary school went to North Myrtle Beach Junior High. It was quite a transition, making all new friends, getting into the routine of junior high school and such exciting new things as changing classes! We all felt so mature in our blue eyeshadow, pink lipstick and nail polish (which I dutifully changed every night before bed) to match our outfits, and mascara.

It was 1969 and everyone else all over the country seemed to be getting into drugs or protesting the war—at least it looked that way on TV—but none of that seemed to affect our town. A few kids were drinking now and then, but no one knew anybody who'd even tried pot. We had no real worries. In fact, for my new friend Judy Joiner and me our most pressing concern was our still flat chests. We each sent away for the Mark Eden bust developer and did our "exercises" every night, all the while praying they would work. As it turned out, though, I was just a late bloomer.

I held a couple of summer jobs, did a lot of babysitting, and even worked for Momma, helping her prepare tax returns. I saved most of my money for school clothes and spent the rest on records. I'd buy a couple of my favorite 45s—Elton John's "Tiny Dancer," the Monkees' "I'm a Believer," Steam's "Na Na Hey Hey Kiss Him Good-bye," and Cream's "White Room"—and play them over and over and over.

I was interested in boys—as always—but still too shy to do much about it. After I got settled in at my new school, I had more friends than ever. The whole bunch of us would go out in groups; Sundays were spent at the movies, no matter what was playing, while Tuesdays and Saturdays were for roller skating. I was a cheerleader and always in on just about every extracurricular activity the school offered, like making the tissue-paper floats for the homecoming. What was the most exciting thing back then? Having the cutest boy (of the day) look at me, an insignificant gesture that would warrant a hopeful mention in my diary and keep me in daydreams until the next possibility came along—usually next week. In early January I "broke up" with a boy I liked. It must have been quite intense since I noted in my diary: "He almost started crying. . . . My nose runny and I keep sniffling." Or maybe I had a cold. Then a boy I liked asked me out for a date, but I turned him down. I was still too young for the real thing.

I made good grades through both seventh and eighth grades—as usual, without much effort. I was becoming more interested in my appearance, dumping my little pixie cut for something cooler, like shoulder-length straight hair. My parents were working as hard as always. Before I knew it, junior high was over and it was summer.

I remember the summer of 1971 especially clearly because so many things happened. I was having a good time that year—coming in as a finalist in the Sun Fun Festival (a local annual celebration) bubble gum–blowing contest and entering the cracker-whistling competition. On this same eventful day I decided that I liked a guy, but my hopes of a serious romance were dashed when I found out that he already had a girlfriend. Four days later, though, he noticed me too. I wrote in my diary: "You wouldn't believe what happened! I made out with that guy I like!!! That's not all he tried to do with me, but I stopped him, of course!" I liked having fun, but I was a responsible girl, even at that young age, and a bit demure as this later entry shows: "I kissed this guy named Carl. I mean, he kissed me." Then in August I began—and ended—my cigarette smoking phase. Sure, it looked cool, but it tasted awful and I decided it just wasn't for me.

But not everything was so lighthearted. Late one Saturday morning Momma told me that she wanted to talk to me about something. Daddy and Chip had gone out in the car for a ride, and all I could think about was that maybe I was in trouble, or that Chip might be getting a hamburger. Momma and I had frequent and frank discussions about important things, like the facts of life. At fourteen I felt that she'd told me just about all there was to know. I couldn't imagine what else could be left, but I could tell from the look on Momma's face that she had something quite serious on her mind. She lit up her usual Pall Mall, poured herself another cup of black instant coffee with sugar, and sat down beside me in the living room.

"Vanna Marie," she began slowly, "what I have to tell you is not going to change anything. You're fourteen years old, and you're grown-up enough to understand what I'm going to say." I wondered what I'd done wrong, because Momma only called me Vanna Marie when I was in serious trouble.

She paused for a long minute, then continued, "Daddy is not your real father."

"What do you mean, Momma?" It all seemed too bizarre. How could the only daddy I had ever known not be my real father?

"A long time ago, I was married to a man named Mike Rosich, for a short time. He is your real father."

I didn't know what to say; I didn't even know what to think. The first questions that popped out of my mouth were, "Is he alive? Where is he? And Chip—is he my real brother or not?"

Momma put her arms around me and held me tight. "Your father lives near New York City. He has another wife now, and they have a little girl who's just a couple of years younger than you. Would you like to meet him?"

I could see how difficult this had been for Momma,

and I didn't want to disappoint her. She was reading my face for clues to what I was really thinking. I thought for a moment. Did I really want to meet a person who, until just a few moments ago, I didn't even know existed? My first thoughts were that I didn't really want to meet him, that my life was fine just the way it was. How could he love me more than Daddy? But then my curiosity took over. What would he look like? Did I look like him? Did I have his eyes, his lips, his skin tone? I really wanted to know, but I was afraid.

"Will you go with me?" I asked Momma.

"Of course," she replied. "You and Chip and I can fly up to New York and visit for a while. We'll make it a vacation."

"All right," I agreed, still not totally convinced that this was what I wanted to do. The funny thing is that instead of wanting to know more about my real father and my mother, the questions that kept coming to mind were all about Chip.

"Is Chip really my brother?"

"Yes, darling. Daddy is his daddy, and I'm his Momma. Nothing has changed."

Momma then explained all about her first marriage: how she'd met my father, when they got married, where they lived, what things were like when I was born, and how things hadn't worked out—that it's possible to love someone very much and yet still not be able to live with them. She also told me about meeting Daddy and how he'd adopted me before

Chip was born, legally changing my last name from Rosich to White. Some kids might have felt resentful toward their parents for hiding these facts, but that feeling never crossed my mind. I trusted my parents, and Momma explained that she'd wanted to tell me the truth many times before but couldn't do it until she was sure that I would understand it. She made the right decision, but no matter how old you are, news like that is hard to take.

Much to her credit, Momma never said a bad word against my father, even though theirs was not the greatest marriage and, after they broke up, Momma often had to go to extremes—like traveling all the way to New York—to collect child support payments. She trusted me to deal with this revelation and come to my own conclusions.

Stunned, I ate lunch with Momma and waited for Daddy and Chip to return. It turned out that the purpose of their little excursion was so that Daddy could tell Chip what Momma had told me. Whatever worries I had about whether or not my true "status" would bother Chip were dispelled when he said of the news, "So what? Vanna's still my sister, so who cares?"

We planned to leave for New York in August, and as the date of our departure drew near, I began to have second thoughts. Chip was looking forward to his first plane ride, and Momma was anxious to see New York again. I was excited too—this was going to be my first flight and the first time I'd seen a place as big as New York City—but more and more I felt torn between wanting to know everything about my father and wanting to also know that nothing had changed with Daddy. In my young mind, these two desires seemed in conflict. I wondered how Daddy would feel if I loved my real father. Would he be hurt? On the day in mid-August when Daddy took the three of us to the airport, I hugged him especially hard, just so he would know how much I loved him, no matter who my real father was.

As our plane made the final approach to New York, I turned to Momma and asked, "What do I call him?"

Without a moment's hesitation, she replied, "Call him Mike."

When we landed at La Guardia Airport, just outside Manhattan, on Long Island, Mike, his wife, Irma, and their daughter, Ingrid, met us. I was stunned when I first saw my father. I could not take my eyes off him. We had the same skin tone, the same features, some of the same gestures, the same eyes. He was handsome, tall, muscular, slim, and very debonair. It was frightening, yet comforting, to see that we looked so much alike. It was also nice to know that he cared about me.

They drove us to the Holiday Inn on West 57th Street, but because our reservations had been messed up, we ended up staying at the old Taft Hotel on Seventh Avenue. At first sight, New York City struck me as very crowded, kind of old and run-down, and dirty. Also, everyone seemed to be moving so quickly.

The following morning Mike picked us up, and we drove out of Manhattan and north, past the Bronx, to White Plains, an upper-middle-class Westchester County suburb. Mike took us to where he lived so that we could meet my natural paternal grandparents, Carlos and Gloria Rosich. As we entered the apartment building lobby, I began to get nervous, and for a moment I thought about how weird it felt to be around my blood relatives who were total strangers.

Irma answered the door. She seemed to be a nice, very outgoing person. Ingrid, who was just a few years younger than me, was watching television in the living room. Everyone was very friendly to one another. They all looked so calm, but my heart was pounding as Irma showed us into the kitchen where my real grandparents sat. Neither of my grandparents could speak English, but their smiles were so warm and welcoming that I relaxed immediately.

Irma served us a wonderful lunch, and I began to feel very much at home, especially after I found that my "new" half sister and I had so much in common. The next day Momma, Chip, Mike, Irma, Ingrid, Gloria, Carlos, and I went to the Statue of Liberty. As we strolled around Liberty Island, I held my grandmother's hand very tightly. At one point, looking down at her sandals, I noticed that her toes were just like mine. They were—and still are—my least favorite feature. Still, it was sort of reassuring to know where I got them.

During our week in New York City we hit all the tourist attractions—the Bronx Zoo, Chinatown, the Empire State Building, Radio City Music Hall, and the NBC tour at Rockefeller Center. It goes without saying that New York City was unlike anything Chip or I had ever experienced and we didn't really know what to make of it. It was huge and beautiful and glamorous, but also hot and sticky and dirty. Of all the sights, my favorite was our visit to NBC, where we watched a taping of the TV game show *Concentration,* with Hugh Downs. Everything on the set looked so different from what you saw on television. I found it fascinating, and that only added to my desire to be on TV someday.

I loved the trip but was very happy to get back to the comfort of home. I was a typical teenager. I'd gone steady and worn the senior key or high school ring of a couple guys. I'd also had my share of adventures, like drinking Boone's Farm apple wine and—no surprise—getting drunk. And I was immersed in worrying about school, gossip, what clothes to wear, what new makeup to try, and getting summer jobs. My parents thought it important that Chip and I have responsibilities outside the home, so we had jobs whenever we could.

That fall I became very interested in religion. In October of 1971 I wrote in my diary that I'd attended a revival meeting at the First Baptist Church and that I'd decided that I wanted to be "saved." Two weeks later I wrote: "Went to a youth meeting at church. I was reborn and it's great!" Lots of my friends were also becoming more active in church, and my parents were very supportive of me in this. Several months later I traveled to Dallas with seventy-three other kids for a Billy Graham rally at the Cotton Bowl. For one week all we did was study the Bible, and I loved every minute of it. I saw God as a powerful and loving entity, and I felt good knowing that he was watching over me. I prayed all the time.

Within the year my interest in the Christian youth movement waned, but though I do not attend church on a regular basis, I still believe in and read the Bible. I just don't proselytize. I think that what's most important is that you have a good heart and that you treat people fairly and honestly. "Do unto others" was the guiding rule in our house. Our parents lived it, and Chip and I learned from their example.

As we got older, our parents continued raising us with the same evenhanded, honest approach. They were strict, but they were also open-minded and realistic about things. For example, if we were curious about alcohol, they'd let us take a sip at home with them. Other parents would just forbid their kids to even try it; then, of course, the kids would be more determined than ever to go out and try it on their own. Now, this is not to say that my parents' attitude toward drinking, for example, kept me from drinking out of the house on my own; it didn't. I experimented with my friends, but at least I had the advantage of what my parents had taught me at home, and I think that made a big difference. When your parents have the kind of attitude ours did, it takes the rebellion factor out of sneaking around, and I think that's half the thrill for most kids. Also, my parents recognized and accepted the fact that they couldn't really protect us from everything or keep us from doing anything. All they could do was teach us about life as best they could and trust us to do the right thing.

That fall I started high school and was thrilled to find out that it was a whole new world. (I've always loved anything that was new or different.) For one thing, there were lots of boys—older boys. And second, for the first time ever, I had to study a subject I absolutely hated—algebra. But, reading my diary, it's clear that I was still a very happy kid. In my last entry for 1971 I wrote: "I thought this was the best year of my life, instead of last year, but next year will be even better." (Did I mention that I am an optimist too?)

My freshman year was pretty uneventful, and except for getting braces—a real trauma at fifteen and a half—things were great. Of course, I had some new boyfriends, including one, Charles Edward Richards, or Hedge, as he was known, who actually kissed me on the Fourth of July—braces and all! In the spring I'd made the cut and was a varsity cheerleader. What more could I want? That summer I worked as a soda jerk at Macelelven's, where I learned to make the world's greatest egg salad, about five dozen eggs' worth a day.

During my sophomore year, I kept busy with the drama club, the student advisory committee, cheerleading, and being class treasurer. Every day I'd sit in class, just waiting for school to end. There was always something else to do. I also had my first really serious boyfriend, Cary Stoffel. He was one year older than me and a star football player. I was in love with him, so of course he didn't like me because I was chasing him. I've always gone after what I wanted, and I really wanted Cary. We didn't have what you'd call a real strong relationship, but I think he liked me. Maybe it took a while because I was just too easy; I'd deprived him of the thrill of the chase.

That February I entered the Miss North Myrtle Beach High School pageant. I didn't win but had lots of fun. And for my sixteenth birthday Daddy and Momma gave me a car. I had a choice—either an Opel GT or a silver VW. Even then I took letters seriously: I chose the VW because those are my initials.

In 1973 Momma learned after a routine examination that she had cancer of the uterus. She had a hysterectomy, and though she recovered very quickly and was soon back at her job selling real estate, she hated being sick even for a minute. I was scared to death for her. I understood that her cancer had been caught early and that her prognosis was very good.

Still, the word *cancer* terrified me. We were closer than ever, and I confided in her a lot. Momma was straight with everyone, but she still kept lots of things inside. As close as you could be to her, she didn't always let you know what she was thinking.

Around the time of her operation she took me aside and said, "Vanna Marie, I don't expect you to be a virgin when you get married, but you'd better be choosy about your men."

I was dumbfounded and, frankly, kind of embarrassed. It was as if Momma had read my mind. I hadn't done anything yet, but like all girls that age, I knew other girls who had. I guess it goes without saying that it seemed like that was all most boys ever thought about. All I could muster was an indignant "Momma!"

She also said, "I want you to take the pill. I don't want you to ruin your life by getting pregnant." I was amazed, and kind of relieved. Even though Momma's style was a lot different from most parents', she was living in the real world, and I knew that while she probably wasn't thrilled at the thought of me becoming sexually active, she loved me enough to look at the situation realistically and try to do what was best for me. By the end of that summer, I had gotten quite serious about Cary. Needless to say, Momma's instincts were correct. As with most things, though I wasn't a perfect kid, I was responsible.

One of the most interesting things about Momma was her interest in psychic phenomena. I didn't realize until I was several years older that my mother wasn't the only person who had experienced things that cannot be explained scientifically or with strict logic. Many people have had psychic experiences— for example, knowing that someone close to you is in trouble, or sensing that someone who has died is still, in some way, "with you." I believe now that we are all psychic to some degree but that some of us welcome these experiences, while others fear them and shut them out.

Although she never made a big deal of it, Momma was without question very psychic. After her mother died, she told me of several times when Grandmama would come to her in what you'd describe as a ghost form—it was like she was really there—to warn her of some impending problem. Once, when I was in my early teens, I suddenly sat up in bed in the middle of the night and looked across the hall and into the bathroom. There, to my shock, I saw Grandmama staring at me, just smiling. It was very comforting, but also frightening. Momma would see Grandmama too, but she took it all in stride. For me, it was enough to know that Grandmama was looking over me; seeing her "materialize" disturbed me. Even today I can accept the idea that deceased loved ones communicate to us, either directly or through mediums, but I have no desire to see them. It's just too unsettling for me.

Once, when I was about seventeen, I went to a bar called the Magic Carpet, a place I was forbidden to go. There were rumored to be lots of drugs available there, and the clientele was considered, at least by my parents, undesirable. I knew better but I went anyway. While I was there, I noticed a strangely dressed woman sitting in the corner. She spoke to no one, and no one else seemed to notice her. She looked like a gypsy of some sort. I thought she was kind of weird, but I forgot about it.

When I got home, Momma met me at the door and said, "Vanna Marie, I told you not to go to that Magic Carpet."

I was stunned. Like just about every place in North Myrtle Beach, the Magic Carpet wasn't very far from my house. Momma hadn't gone out all evening. For some reason I blurted out, "I knew that was you in the corner dressed up like a gypsy." But when I really thought about it, I knew that that didn't make sense either. Momma didn't do any such thing. She wasn't there. But somehow she knew that I was. Like Grandmama, Momma also had precognitive dreams; in other words, she knew ahead of time when things were going to happen. You could just tell by a look Momma had or her tone of voice.

Not content to await Grandmama's unpredictable visits, Momma got into the Ouija board. She and I would each put both hands on the ivory plastic pointer, and within seconds it would be moving swiftly from letter to letter and to the "Yes" and "No" spots on the board. Momma would ask questions and Grandmama would answer. Though Momma took the Ouija board business quite seriously, I was a little bit skeptical about it. After all, the Ouija board is sold as a game, and I secretly suspected that we were unconsciously "guiding" the pointer. One day I sat down with it alone and closed my eyes. It moved, and when I looked after each stop, I saw that the message did make sense. After that I was never really comfortable doing the board, and eventually I stopped altogether.

In 1974, my junior year of high school, I was student council vice president and a member of the Honor Society. I was still a cheerleader and had once again come in runner-up in the Miss North Myrtle Beach High School pageant. That summer I'd also been in the Sun Fun pageant but hadn't won that one either. I lost interest in Cary and fell in love with Jimmy Riddle, tried pot for the first time (and hated it), and made my dramatic debut in our class production of *A Portrait of Jenny*.

School was still fun, but as I went through my senior year, I thought about the decisions I'd have to make in the upcoming months. Where I lived, the next step after high school was usually marriage. North Myrtle Beach was still a small town that only a handful of kids ever left. Most of my girlfriends had been filling their hope chests, making wedding plans, and thinking about having babies before we had even graduated. This is what most of us expected to do, as evidenced by some of the inscriptions in my yearbook—things like, "It has been nice knowing you and going to school with you. I wish you the best of luck in your married life"; and from one of my girlfriends, "I can't wait until about ten years from now. Just think, all of us will probably be married by then with a few kids running around." Jimmy and I had been going together for some time and I was wearing his high school ring, and I did think about marrying him. I know that if I had married him and raised a family there, I would have been happy, *if* I were certain that that was what I wanted. But I wasn't, and as always, Momma seemed to sense what was going on.

The night before I graduated, Momma and I went off by ourselves and had a long talk. Once we started talking, there was no stopping us, and though we'd talked a lot before, this conversation was very different. She told me of her own hopes and dreams, some of which surprised me. I never knew until then that my mother and I shared the same dream, to go to Hollywood and make it in show business. After that I realized that Momma lived through me vicariously. And that evening she told me things that she'd learned in her life, things that I still think about now and then and that have helped me ever since.

When we talked about whether I should get married or go to modeling school in Atlanta, as I'd planned, she said, "You know, you can get married now and have kids and be very happy. But ten years from now, you may wonder what it would have been like if you'd gone to school, and whether or not you could have made it. Or maybe you'll wish you'd seen a big city like Los Angeles, or maybe Europe. You make your own decisions, and we will back you, no matter what you decide. But keep in mind that you can always get married after you've done everything. You don't have to do it right now."

It dawned on me then that despite all of my mother's hard work and accomplishments, she did have some regrets, that there were some things that she'd wished she had done. For the first time, Momma and I were really friends, a relationship that endured for the rest of her life.

4

I spent the summer after graduation working and getting ready to go to modeling school in Atlanta in the fall. The more I thought about moving to Atlanta, the more excited I was. My long-term goal was to move to Los Angeles, but I knew that I wasn't quite ready for that. I saw Atlanta as a good transitional, or jumping-off, point.

My girlfriend Debbie Brown was attending a fashion school in Miami as part of her training to become a hairdresser, and when she told me what she'd learned there, I decided that a similar school might be the answer for me. I had no desire to attend a regular four-year college and work toward a degree. While

I had always done extremely well in school, the prospect of four more years of hitting the books just didn't appeal to me. I really wanted to be a model, so I sent away for brochures from all the leading schools. The Atlanta School of Fashion and Design was only three hundred miles from home, and after Daddy, Momma, and I visited the school and talked with some people there in late April, I decided that it was for me.

One Saturday in late September, we loaded up the station wagon and my VW and drove to Atlanta. Before we were even out of state, I became homesick. Though I knew that I'd be only six hours' drive away and that I could come home whenever I wanted, I felt like I was moving to the end of the world. When we got into Atlanta that afternoon, we checked into a hotel about two miles from school, then took a drive around the area and went out to dinner.

The next day we drove over to the school and there got directions to the Red Lion, a nearby apartment house complex that served as "dorms" for the out-of-town students. When we got there, we discovered that my three roommates, Yvonne, Mimi, and Sandy, were already settled in. The four us were to share a two-bedroom, one-bath, furnished apartment. Each bedroom had a pair of twin beds; Yvonne and Mimi shared one room, and Sandy and I shared the other. They seemed like nice girls, and I was anxious to unpack and get things organized. Momma helped me put everything away while Daddy fiddled around in the kitchen, unplugging the garbage disposal and unjamming a stuck window. By the time we were finished, it was dinnertime, and so Daddy treated everyone, including my new roommates, to dinner. It was a lot of fun, and by the time the evening was over, I was pretty sure that we'd all get along fine.

Classes started that Monday, promptly at noon. Momma and Daddy joined me for breakfast before they left for South Carolina. Saying good-bye to my parents is something I will always remember. It was especially hard, knowing that I wouldn't see Momma every day. To make things even more difficult, she was probably more upset than me. Now I was officially on my own. I knew I'd really miss my folks, and I even composed this poem for Daddy:

> *When I was very young*
> *Was when it all began.*
> *My mother fell in love*
> *With a fantastic man.*
>
> *He soon became my father*
> *And raised me like his own.*
> *I have loved him so dearly,*
> *More than he's ever known.*
>
> *Through all these changing years,*
> *He's coped with all my fears.*
> *And even more than that,*
> *He's dried all of my tears.*

> *Words cannot explain*
> *How thankful to God I am*
> *For giving me such a father*
> *Who really gives a damn.*

At first glance, school looked like it was going to be a breeze. I mean, how much work is it to learn how to be a model? To learn how to pose? And walk? Looking back, I see that though I'd come to the school with a lot of ambition and drive, I knew less about what I'd be doing there than I thought. Before too long I realized that this was like any other school. Classes started at nine o'clock every morning, lasted until eleven-thirty, when we took an hour-long lunch break, then resumed until five in the afternoon. Generally speaking, this was not a school for models but for people who wanted to study design and merchandising. As I'd later learn, there's really no school that can teach you how to be a model. A school might be able to prepare you in terms of learning about fashion, makeup, and poise, but you can learn the business only by doing. I was required to study merchandising, the history of fashion, and design, from the Victorian era to the present. There was also a lot of reading to do and papers to write, but very little actual modeling.

As far as I knew, all of the students were women. One day I remarked about how great another girl looked, and someone corrected me, saying it was "he" not "she." I learned then that one of my classmates was in fact a male who came to class every day in drag. I was so naïve, I'd never heard of such a thing.

It wasn't long before I was feeling a little discouraged. I was so anxious to start modeling and felt that I was really wasting my time with classes. Besides, if my modeling career hadn't taken off, I probably would have gone into real estate, not any other aspect of the fashion industry. That's not to say that I didn't learn a lot while I was there; there were classes that taught us the ins and outs of dressing, makeup, poise, and so on. But I could have learned much of this either on my own or at a finishing school. And realizing all this made me feel less than happy about the fact that my parents were paying five thousand dollars a year in tuition for me to learn things that I would probably never use.

I began to feel depressed, and I spent a lot of time talking to Momma on the phone. She was then running for a seat on the city council and was quite busy, though never so busy that she didn't have time to listen to all my problems. My feelings of homesickness hadn't gone away. Momma assured me that my feelings were perfectly normal—after all, I was out on my own for the first time. She encouraged me to ride it out, but it just got harder instead of easier.

I made friends with my roommates. One was a very demure southern girl, while the other two were rather wild. I smoked some pot with the two wilder girls and came home with such an intense case of the munchies that I ate an entire meatloaf. I knew that I couldn't go on like that much longer if I expected to be a model. But aside from the occasional misadventure, I stayed out of trouble. I was a good kid; I knew the difference between right and wrong.

My new friends and I would hit the discos on weekend nights. Down South, discos were all the rage, and we thought it cool to be seen at places like the Electric Ballroom, Bogart's, T.J.'s, the Library, Kelly's, and the Colorado Mining Company. We always traveled in a group because it was more fun and, frankly, a lot safer. Though Atlanta wasn't New York City or Los Angeles, it was still the biggest city any of us had ever been in, and we were all a little less worldly than we liked to think. I'm sure some men saw college girls, especially those from the fashion school, as "hits." If someone bothered any of us, it was easier to leave as a group.

Within a few weeks of school starting, I noticed that we kept running into this gorgeous man in the clubs. He had blue eyes and blond hair, wore lots of jewelry, was well dressed, and though I could see that he was much older than I, I was very attracted to him. We would say hello to each other in passing—that was all, until a friend introduced us to each other on Halloween night at the Mining Company. His name was Gordy Watson.

The next time I ran into him, about a week later, we spent the whole evening just talking at a small corner table. I learned that he was about fifteen years older than I, had three children, and was divorced. He made a very comfortable living selling luxury cars—Rolls-Royces, Ferraris, Mercedes-Benzes, Jaguars, and others—through his dealership in Atlanta. That evening I went home with him. I can honestly say that this was a case of love at first sight. Usually I take my time and don't always act so impulsively. But when it came to Gordy, I literally could not control my emotions. It was the beginning of a very serious and intense relationship that would last over the next four years. Two weeks later Gordy introduced me to his three kids. They were adorable, and I enjoyed being around them.

After I'd been in school five weeks, I was going on modeling interviews, even though I still didn't have a professional book, or portfolio. I did my first professional modeling job in early November at the Atlanta Merchandise Mart. I can't remember exactly what company it was for, but I modeled the different outfits for their new spring line. I was very excited about making thirty-five dollars a day and getting to keep some of the clothes I modeled.

Between school, modeling, and spending a lot of time with Gordy, I started to feel that I was burning the candle at both ends. I made a conscious effort to take better care of myself than I had. There was no way I could go out drinking with my friends all night and then get up for an eight-o'clock class the next morning; not to mention trying to look great for modeling jobs. The camera never lies.

Momma had met Gordy in November when she came to Atlanta to visit me. I worried that she wouldn't like the idea of me seeing a man so much older, but to my surprise she just told me that she felt more comfortable knowing that I was being taken care of in the "big city." Daddy felt the same way, although he always had a vague fear that I might somehow become involved in the drug scene. He needn't have worried, though. I knew from the start that there were some things I really didn't want to do.

By Christmas I was madly in love with Gordy. I spent the holiday in North Myrtle Beach with my family, and on Christmas Eve, after returning home from a candlelight church service, I opened the two presents from Gordy. One was a beautiful diamond and emerald ring, and the other was a diamond necklace. Momma had to scrape me off the ceiling.

This was no high school romance. Gordy was unlike anyone I'd ever met. He was very kind and thoughtful, with a sort of genteel southern manner. He was also quite worldly. He'd been around and knew a great deal about life and people. I not only loved him, I really liked him and enjoyed doing all kinds of things together, even just sitting home and watching television. Even though we went out to nightclubs often, Gordy was actually somewhat conservative and domestic. We spent many evenings at home, often with his children.

During that vacation I visited all my friends and then headed back to Atlanta in my silver VW. Thirty or so miles west of home, I got into a serious accident. The car was totaled, but luckily I was unhurt. I called home and Momma and Daddy came to get me. The next day they drove me back to Atlanta, promising they would find me another car. A week or so later, Daddy drove the three hundred miles to Atlanta with my "new" car—a three-year-old black Cutlass with burgundy interior. I rarely used that car, since I usually took one of Gordy's, but I liked having it around. It reminded me of home.

With just a few modeling assignments under my belt—and having decided that I absolutely hated school—I went home to North Myrtle Beach for the summer. My plan was to make as much money as I could working over the summer and return to Atlanta in the fall, get my own apartment, and with a good chunk of savings in the bank, pursue modeling full-time. I also used the summer to think about my relationship with Gordy. It had all happened so quickly, I needed to reassure myself that it was real. Back home, I got a well-paying job as a cocktail waitress at a local resort. I also entered the Sun Fun Festival beauty pageant. The girls I was competing against were all friends of mine, and we had a wonderful time participating in the parade and the pageant. But—as always, it seemed—I came in second runner-up.

By August, when I returned to Atlanta, I knew that I really wanted to be with Gordy. My plans to find a place of my own were shelved when Gordy asked me to come live with him. I discussed it with my parents, and they told me that I was old enough to make my own decisions and whatever I decided was all right with them. I moved into Gordy's three-story house on Ragley Hall Road. It was a very modern, luxurious home. After a summer spent without him, it was wonderful to be back in his arms. Though we hadn't really made plans, I was pretty sure that we would marry each other someday.

As for my career, things seemed to be really looking up. I needed an agent to help me get more modeling work, so I picked one out of the phone book. I got all dressed up, went to Atlanta Models and Talent, Inc., and met with Kathy Hardegree. They took me on as a client and gave me a list of test photographers who would do the photos for my portfolio. I went to one of the photographers, who took several different kinds of shots, each designed to show how I would look in different settings. There was a "glamour" shot in high-fashion clothes and full makeup, a natural shot that was used mainly for commercials, a bikini shot to show off the body, and a couple others. These were all put together on a composite sheet, which also included my name and vital statistics, and this sheet would be sent out by my agent to potential clients. Having the photos and composites made up cost several hundred dollars, and keeping up a good wardrobe also cost money, but my career took off so quickly and my living expenses were so low that I could concentrate on modeling exclusively.

Within a few weeks of signing with my agent, I auditioned for—and got—a part in an industrial film, where I played a sexy secretary. This was my first film assignment and I loved it. Two days later I got a local commercial for Mitchell Motors, an Atlanta Oldsmobile dealer. I was very lucky to do as well as I did.

The modeling field in Atlanta and in other areas of the country outside New York and L.A. is a good place to start. For one thing, these "outside" markets aren't as specific about their requirements, and that can be a big help. In my case, being only five foot six would have been a definite hindrance if I'd gone straight to New York, where most models have to be at least five foot eight or so. And even though I weighed only ten or fifteen pounds more than I do now, it seemed that it all settled in my bust. Even though I was a late developer, by the time I'd "blossomed," I was very busty for a model. In fact, unless you're modeling lingerie or wedding gowns, the fashion world has very little use for a woman who is not on the "flat" side.

My best features were my legs, hands (which I inherited from Momma), and hair. Most people starting out in modeling see themselves only in layouts in *Vogue,* when, in fact, there's a great deal of money to be made from just your "parts." For example, in the beginning I made up to $150 an hour hand modeling, where you saw only my hand gripping a soda can, bearing fine jewelry, or running over a piece of luxurious carpeting. Once I made $1,000 for one day of hand modeling—I couldn't believe it. It sounds easy, but it can actually be quite tedious as you repeat the same gesture for hours on end. I remember getting finished with the soda ad and wondering if my fingers would ever straighten out again. But that was my job!

Other jobs called on me to do print and catalog work, posing in clothes for ads that ran in the *Atlanta Constitution* for stores such as Rich's (I also did their seasonal catalogs). In one ad I might look very sexy, wearing beautiful diamond jewelry, while in another I'd have my hair up in a matronly bun and be wearing a pretty, middle-aged-type shirtdress so that I could look like everybody's mom for a Mother's Day sale. I also posed for ads that ran in such national magazines as *Vogue, Mademoiselle, Harper's Bazaar,* and *Cosmopolitan,* including one for a food product that promised to increase your bust size.

Another thing models do is work conventions, of which there were many in Atlanta. In my four years there, I worked for Truck-Lite, Hercules, Joshua Tree, Scotch-Guard, Raytheon Data Systems, the American Booksellers Association (where, interestingly enough, I'll be again—but this time as an author), and Exxon. For Exxon I wore a tiger costume, complete with a hood and tiger ears and a long tail that

These are the only photos I have
of my mother and me with
my father, Mike Rosich.
After he left, we moved in with
my Grandma and Grandpa Nicholas
(top right).

In 1959, Momma married Herbert Stackley White
(always Daddy to me) and one year later,
my baby brother, Chip, was born.

At my sophomore prom, thrilled to be wearing my first formal gown.

Daddy and me at the annual Father/Daughter Church Supper.

June 12

1971

Dear Diary,

Today is a terrible day. Judy came over and we went to the park for Old Fashioned Day concerning Sun Fun. I entered the bubble gum blowing and was a finalist. I also entered the cracker whisleing contest but egh_ Well, here comes the bad part. I went skating and you know I like Chucky, well, this girl was flirting with him, her name was Susan. Then I saw them wall down to the beach together! Help!

72'

Dear Diary,

I am now in Dallas Texas learning about Jesus Christ. It is fantastic. All 74 of us are there. The 15 Chicks I went to Holiday Inn North Lange. Band (Cold Steel)

I started keeping a diary when I was in junior high, mainly to record the ups and downs of my teenage romances.

Being a cheerleader
taught me the
tools of my trade:
how to smile
and how to point.

Here I am competing
for the title of
"Miss Fire Prevention."

I'm looking better
here on a float in
the Sun Fun Parade.

In 1973, at my junior prom with my date, Joey Edge.

One year later, I attended my senior prom with Jimmy Riddle, the second love of my life.

Even before I left home
and became a model,
I was always posing.
I guess I thought I looked
pretty sexy with my long
eyelashes and glass of
wine (both fake!)

One of my first,
though certainly
not favorite,
modeling shots.

Although I was too short (5′6″) and busty to meet New York modeling standards, my career in Atlanta took off almost immediately.

In 1978, at age 21, I entered the Miss Georgia Universe Beauty Pageant.

As you can see, I didn't win.

Christopher George, another Myrtle Beach native,
was my first mentor and true friend in L.A.

On the set of *Midnight Offerings* with
Melissa Sue Anderson.

I came to L.A. to do movies or television, but it was modeling assignments that helped pay the rent.

(PHOTO BY LENNON)

John and me on our very first real date
on Christmas Eve, 1981.

John took great pride in his car and got a kick out of its license plate.

Here I am, looking a lot tamer than John.

(PHOTO BY ALISON REYNOLDS)

Some of our happiest times together were spent at John's parents' lakefront house in Michigan.

My life changed on Thanksgiving Eve, 1982,
with a phone call from the producer of
Wheel of Fortune announcing
"You've got the job!"

People often say Pat and I look like a
brother-sister team. (PHOTO BY RON SLENZAK)

Pat plays straight man
to my cheerleader.

(PHOTOS BY RON SLENZAK)

Although you may only see Pat and me on the set, there are dozens of people in the "Wheel" family, all who work terribly hard to pull the show together.

(PHOTO BY CHARLES BUSH)

(PHOTOS BY RON SLENZAK)

"Do I get to keep the clothes I wear on the show?" is the question I'm most often asked. Turn the page to see the real me, dressed in clothes selected from my own closet.

Arriving at NBC for a long day of taping.

On a typical day of taping, I change my hair, make-up, accessories, and clothes five times. Talk about feeling like a Barbie doll.

(PHOTOS BY RON SLENZAK)

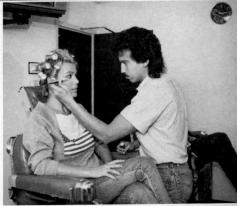

Bruce Grayson making me pretty.

My wardrobe mistress, Florence Calce, and I have some hard decisions to make for each show.

Jack Clark and me
warming up the audience
before the show begins.

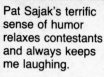

Pat Sajak's terrific
sense of humor
relaxes contestants
and always keeps
me laughing.

I love my job and I guess it shows!
(PHOTO BY RON SLENZAK)

"Teasing" the prizes is what these graceful hand and arm gestures are referred to in the trade.
(PHOTO BY RON SLENZAK)

On *The Johnny Carson Show* in Fall 1986.
(PHOTO BY WENDY PERL)

With Jonn Stossel, taping a *20/20* segment about
Wheel of Fortune.

My fans mean
a lot to me.
(above) A special
greeting from the
Evanston, Illinois
Fire Department.
(below) With
Willard Scott and
my most loyal fan,
John Redmann,
a college student
who comes to
almost every
taping.

(PHOTO BY DAN GOLDEN)

I feel best when I work out or jog every day, but recently, all I have time for is a morning routine of sit-ups and push-ups.

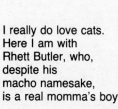

I really do love cats.
Here I am with
Rhett Butler, who,
despite his
macho namesake,
is a real momma's boy.

(PHOTO BY ROGER KARNBAD)

Crocheting is
my favorite hobby.

I'm really a homebody at heart.

On Christmas 1985, our last together, John surprised me with a fur jacket . . .

. . . and a new robe and fluffys.

One of the last
photographs taken of
John and me together.

Here we are, with
our closest friends,
my manager,
Ray Manzella,
and his wife,
Sondra.

For my first poster, I decided to pose in my favorite clothes — my jeans. (PHOTO BY LISA O'CONNOR)

My latest poster suggests a whole different mood.
(PHOTO BY CHARLES BUSH)

Here I am today, showing my many faces. As you can see, most are pretty happy.

(PHOTOS BY HARRY LANGDON)

I tripped over a couple of times. It was gratifying to know that I was being noticed by people outside Atlanta too. In 1977 I was approached by someone from *Playboy* who asked if I'd like to do a test shoot and be considered for a layout. Of course, I was flattered to have been asked, but I've always been a very private person and, when it comes to some things, actually quite shy. I knew without giving it a moment's thought that posing nude was something I just could never do.

By 1978 my jobs were taking me out of Atlanta. One television commercial for Catalina swimwear was shot at the Fontainebleau Hotel in Miami in February. Now, Miami is warmer than the rest of the country at that time of year, but it's still not warm enough for anyone to spend hour after hour jumping into an ice-cold pool. When I finally saw the commercial, I was surprised that I wasn't blue.

That year I decided to enter the Miss Georgia Universe beauty pageant. At twenty-one I was all excited about it. I always liked pageants, but not just for the idea of winning. Unlike some girls I've seen in pageants, I was never pressured by anyone to compete; in fact, I don't really see pageants as competitions but as opportunities for young women to see if they like modeling and gain some poise. Also, although some people might think this sounds a little corny, you do get to meet a lot of new people, and the weeks of preparation, rehearsal, and judging are fun.

Momma and Daddy came to see the pageant, which was held at the Peachtree Plaza Hotel in Atlanta. Everyone working with the pageant tried to put us at ease, but we were all nervous. In fact, one girl walked right off the runway and fell into the audience. The rest of us couldn't believe it! I felt terrible for her.

There are supposed to be all kinds of "tricks" you can use in a pageant, but the only one I ever used was to coat my teeth and lips with Vaseline. It probably sounds unpleasant, but when you're up there you get so nervous and thirsty, it's the only way to keep your mouth moist. I came in fourth runner-up (again!), but it was a great experience.

Just a few weeks after the pageant, I went on the first of several interviews for small movie parts. One was for the Sally Field movie *Norma Rae*, and another was for the Burt Reynolds film *Smokey and the Bandit*. I also interviewed for a part in the television show *The Dukes of Hazzard*, but none of these jobs came through. Still, the more interviews I went on for acting roles, the more certain I was that acting was where I wanted the modeling to lead. I also realized that I couldn't stay in Atlanta forever. Sooner or later, I'd have to move to Los Angeles. On New Year's Day 1979 I wrote in my diary: "My goal is to really do something big. I know it's probably a childish dream, but I'm going to try to make it come true."

Every time I'd think about leaving Atlanta, I'd have

to think about leaving Gordy. I loved him very much, but our attitudes toward the relationship were different. The main difference of opinion was over monogamy. Though we dated each other exclusively in the beginning, I knew that Gordy liked to spend time with other women. A lot of it was just curiosity. Gordy had married at a very young age and never went out with many different women. Once he was divorced, I guess he felt like it was just something he had to do. But I loved him, and I really wanted the relationship to work. After a particularly difficult period, I went to Las Vegas on a ten-day assignment. While I was away I thought everything over and made my decision: I was leaving Gordy and moving out to L.A.

When I got back to Atlanta and told Gordy what I planned to do, he took back all the gifts he'd given me over the years. He hid everything—including all the Christmas and birthday gifts—and told me that I could have them back if I married him. I said no. Gordy had just broken my heart one too many times. I realized that I needed a change and that I had to leave.

Around Thanksgiving 1979 my friend Belinda Berry and I discussed moving to Los Angeles together. She was also a model and had an adventurous streak. We got along great, so I moved my few things from Gordy's into Belinda's apartment in Atlanta and then went home to spend the holidays with my parents.

By this time Momma and Daddy had long been separated. Apparently their marriage hadn't been good for some time, a fact she and Daddy kept pretty well hidden from Chip and me. They waited until mid-1978, when Chip graduated high school, to separate. Momma was working as a cashier at the Seafarer Restaurant at the local Holiday Inn, and she had her own one-bedroom apartment just a few blocks from the house she'd shared with Daddy.

Momma and Daddy were still on good terms, and she really felt that she was starting over again. She was looking forward to life and was excited about being on her own. One day, while showering, Momma noticed a lump on her right calf and another on her back. She mentioned the lumps to a few close friends and made them promise not to tell anyone. But Polly Lowman and one of Momma's other friends, Libby Owens, insisted that she see a doctor.

Daddy took her to see a doctor, who insisted that she go into the Grand Strand Hospital for exploratory surgery and treatment. The lumps were removed, biopsied, and proved malignant. The surgeon told Daddy that they removed as much cancerous tissue as they could, but there was the possibility that the cancer had metastasized and would show up elsewhere in her body.

Momma went home to recover and was doing well for a while. But suddenly she started losing weight, and her fingers and hands were always swollen. Daddy took her to the Medical University of South Carolina in Charleston, about 110 miles away, for more extensive tests. After five days, it was confirmed that she had lung cancer and needed surgery immediately. I came home from Atlanta to be with her. Chip wanted to come with us, but couldn't take the day off from his job.

I remember lying in the hospital bed alongside her the night before surgery. She smoked her last cigarette right before midnight. We soon fell asleep in each other's arms.

Sometime during the middle of the night, a nurse came in and wrote on Momma's chart, "Mother and daughter sleeping happily." Momma saw the nurse come in the room and couldn't wait to get up and read what she'd written. It was typical of Momma to always want to know everything that was going on.

I seemed to feel everything that Momma felt; we were that close. The morning before the operation we were both very nervous. I held her hand tightly as two hospital orderlies wheeled her down the hall to the operating room. The doctors made a huge incision across her chest that circled under her arm to her back, and removed a large portion of her right lung. During the operation Daddy and I paced the floors, saying little. After several hours, the doctor appeared and told us that the operation had gone smoothly. I gave Daddy a big hug. They took Momma into the intensive care unit, and I waited there for her to wake up.

I cherish a letter Momma wrote to me on July 14,

1979, a short time after the surgery. One part reads: "Vanna, I can never say in person or be able to put on paper what having you with me during my surgery meant. I shall never forget waking up and seeing your smiling face looking at me. I know now why God blessed me with you. I love you more than I can ever show you. When you need me, darlin', I'll be there. As long as I live, I'll never let you down."

Momma knew that I wanted to move to California, and despite everything, her enthusiasm for my plans never waned. She was as excited as if she were going herself. When I returned to North Myrtle Beach for the holidays, I told her that Belinda and I would be going after the first of the year. Momma couldn't have been happier for me. I also told her that, as soon as she felt better, she could come out to Los Angeles and live with me. For the six months after the operation, her health seemed to improve dramatically. She felt great, resumed her job at the Holiday Inn, and was even going out.

On January 2, 1980, before the sun came up, Belinda and I struck out in a twenty-foot rented U-Haul truck. We stopped along the way, first in Memphis, where Belinda's parents lived. The next morning, after staying at her parents' house, we hit the road. Belinda didn't know how to drive a stick shift. Needless to say, she soon learned. She steered and pushed the clutch, while I shifted gears. What a sight! On our fourth day of traveling we drove more than seven hundred miles. When we saw the sign for Palm Springs, we knew Los Angeles wasn't much farther. We arrived in L.A. late that night.

Although I'd dreamed about going to Hollywood for twenty-three years, seeing it was strange. It was different from what I'd expected—full of palm trees and lights, but no glitter or glamour. It was much bigger than I had imagined, but there were also parts of it, like Hollywood Boulevard, that were much tackier than I'd expected. Still, I was just thrilled to have finally arrived. I knew people who lived in the Oakwood Apartments complex in the San Fernando Valley, just a stone's throw from several major television and movie studios. We spent the night with friends, then were at the complex's rental office on Sunday morning with money in hand.

We'd hoped to find a two-bedroom apartment for about four hundred dollars a month and were surprised to find that the best we could do was seven hundred dollars. For that, we got two bedrooms, two baths, and many extras like a pool, health club, and tennis courts. It also turned out to be a great place for young newcomers to live. Art Carney's son Brian lived there, as did Jack Coleman, who plays Steven Carrington on *Dynasty*, John James from *The Colbys*, and Ted McGinley of *Dynasty*. Also, lots of large companies, including NBC, put up employees there when they had to be in town for more than just a few days.

I had one thousand dollars with me when I arrived in Los Angeles. In addition to paying my half of the first and last months' rent, I also needed a car to get around. Through a friend of my family's who lived out there, I discovered Penelope, a white dented Ford Pinto with 100,000 miles on her. (She was named by her previous owner.) There went my last three hundred dollars. I was down to literally counting pennies. Belinda had brought out lots of furniture from her apartment, but I had nothing, not even a bed, so I slept on the floor. It took me about six weeks to save up for a bedroom set that cost two hundred dollars.

Belinda went to work in the passport office, which was the kind of job she was looking for. I wanted to work as a model or on TV, but Los Angeles proved harder to crack than Atlanta. The competition was a lot tougher. You couldn't just walk in and get work, and my financial situation demanded that I find a job, any job. I went to work in an Italian restaurant called Luigi's. A lot of people from the nearby studios would stop there after work or during a dinner break. I even met some celebrities there, including Josh Taylor, one of the stars of *Days of Our Lives*. We became good friends. But even better than meeting people, Luigi's proved to be a great place because they would accommodate me when I needed time off to go on interviews or auditions.

A couple of days after my twenty-third birthday, Josh took me over to the *Days* set to meet some of the other actors. Josh introduced me to the assistant producer, who asked me if I was an actress (I said yes, of course) and insisted I bring by a résumé the next day. *Days of Our Lives* was Momma's favorite daytime soap, so when I told her all this, she nearly fainted. Josh also showed me the studio where Johnny Carson taped the *Tonight* show. After I'd described the *Tonight* show set to Momma in a letter, I wrote: "One day I'll be on there!"

I was also lucky to have among my friends Christopher George and his wife, Lynda Day. Chris and his family had been close to Momma for years, and he often invited me over to dinner. Chris had twenty years' experience in show business, and because he knew Momma, he sort of looked out for me. He was protective of me and offered lots of good advice. One thing I learned from him was that other actors can't really help you get jobs. It's too big a town with too many other struggling hopefuls. One night after dinner he said to me very bluntly, "Vanna, you can't get a job in this town by lying on your back." He'd also let me know in not so subtle ways that I could stand to lose a little weight. I remember him saying, "You have an ass on you, don't you?" His wife Lynda gave me a list of reputable modeling agents to see.

After a few months Belinda decided to move to an apartment closer to where she worked. I got a new roommate, Susan Mechsner, whom I'd met through one of my neighbors, Casey Ortez. She was dating a good friend of Casey's named Ed Lozzi. The four of us went out often, or stayed home and barbecued.

Casey and I were from similar backgrounds and

shared a common goal: to make it in show business. He'd been a football hero in his hometown of Dallas, and he wanted to work as an actor and a stuntman.

I liked him right away, and we dated very steadily. Casey always liked challenges. He would drive fast and was quite a daredevil. This recklessness also included both of us drinking and occasionally doing pot and cocaine. I guess we all go through stages, and at least think about experimenting with drugs. I feel that I'm luckier than many people, because it didn't take me long to satisfy my curiosity and realize that drugs are trouble. You can't be high or sit around procrastinating if you expect to accomplish anything. When the truth of this sunk in, Casey and I eventually went our separate ways. He later moved back to Dallas.

I didn't hear from Casey until one day in May 1982 when I got an unexpected call from him. I didn't know what prompted the call; we hadn't spoken in months or really kept in touch. He was calling from Dallas and he told me how much he appreciated me and how good I was to him. I was touched, but I still didn't quite know what to make of the call. The very next day Casey's sister called to tell me that Casey had hanged himself the night before.

5

I was used to rejection, but I didn't realize that you had to be much more tough-skinned to make it in Hollywood. When things didn't start happening for me as quickly as they had in Atlanta, I felt unsure of myself, depressed, and bored. I wasn't exercising, and out of frustration and unhappiness I started eating. Whole pies, cakes, meatloaves, a dozen doughnuts—anything. Once I polished off an entire cheesecake in one sitting. At that rate it didn't take me very long to balloon up to over 130 pounds, between 20 and 25 pounds above my ideal weight. One day I looked in the mirror and decided that I just couldn't stand it anymore. I looked like a blimp, felt sluggish and tired, and was caught up in a vicious cycle. I was depressed because I didn't have an agent and I wasn't getting jobs. But how could I expect to get an agent or a job if I looked like this?

I would talk to Momma on the phone, but though I'd tell her that things weren't perfect, I never let on just how bad they were. She had enough on her mind without worrying about me.

I knew that dieting was all a matter of mind control. I just woke up one day and said, "This is the day!" I cleaned all the junk food, sweets, and breads out of my cabinets, restocked them with only fresh fruits and vegetables, started exercising, and dropped ten pounds in a flash. As usual, the last fifteen pounds were a little tougher to lose, but I refused to give up. Once I knew that I was well on my way to my goal, I began feeling better about everything.

Before I really got the diet under way, I enrolled in an acting class run by Vincent Chase. I found him through Claire Miller, someone else Chris George had introduced me to. The classes were held every evening from seven in the evening until midnight and cost about one hundred dollars a month. Right near the classroom, on Sunset Boulevard, was a supermarket. Every time we'd take a break, I'd go to the store and buy some other fattening junk food. It was awful. But I was very dedicated to the class; I treated it like a job and worked very hard at learning my scenes and the technique. In the beginning I had the rather naïve idea that acting meant memorizing and delivering lines. I learned very quickly that it takes a lot of effort to make acting look natural. Though I'd taken drama in high school, it was nothing like this. Among my classmates were Ted McGinley, who was then on *Happy Days* and has since appeared on *Dynasty* and *Love Boat*; Brian Patrick Clark from *Eight Is Enough* and *General Hospital*; Leann Hunley, of *Days of Our Lives* and *Dynasty*; and Patrick Cassidy, younger brother of one of my favorite teen idols, David Cassidy. Patrick and I became good friends.

As soon as I had my goal in sight, I started thinking about getting an agent. Working at Luigi's was fine for the time being and it paid the bills, but I hadn't come to Los Angeles to work in a restaurant. I set my sights high: Why not go to see the top Hollywood modeling agent?

One afternoon I drove Penelope into Hollywood, parked her on a side street, and walked into the building on Hollywood Boulevard that housed the Nina Blanchard Agency. Nina, considered one of the sharpest women around and one of the toughest, was in her twentieth year of business when I met her in 1980. Among her clients were Cheryl Tiegs (whom she'd discovered in 1965), Cristina Ferrare, and Christie Brinkley. Today she represents Shari Belafonte-Harper and Catherine Oxenberg.

As you can probably figure out from that roster, Nina was hardly holding her breath waiting for me to come along. In fact, her agency receives about four thousand letters and photos from aspiring models every single week. Of those, only a few are ever invited in for a personal interview. There are a couple hours each week when the agency holds an "open interview," where anyone can walk in off the street and be seen. Usually about six hundred people will show up, and each will be seen for about thirty seconds.

I knew from my experience in Atlanta that modeling agents are very precise and strict about their criteria. And unlike some other people working in the business, they are the very last to offer anyone false hope; it just isn't in their interest. When it comes to modeling, you could say that Nina wrote the book, and it's literally true too. So you can imagine how proud I felt when I learned that I'd passed the initial screening and would be personally interviewed by Nina herself. I was escorted into her office. I remember that the walls were covered by framed magazine covers featuring some of her two hundred clients. There were magazines lying about everywhere it seemed, and the phone never stopped ringing. I had imagined it being a lot more glamorous and plush than it really was.

As I sat down across the desk from Nina, she opened my portfolio of about twenty-five pages. Inside were tearsheets from past modeling assignments as well as 8×10 and 11×14 photographs of me, in both black-and-white and color, and in a variety of different kinds of clothes and settings. My heart was in my throat as she carefully turned each page, slowly looking at every detail of every shot. She smiled, and every few moments would say an approving "uh-huh." I just sat there petrified. Then, as she got to the last page in the leather binder, she asked me matter-of-factly, "How tall are you?"

"Five six," I replied.

In a flash, she slammed my portfolio closed and pushed it across her desk at me. She stopped smiling. "We don't take anyone under five seven. Thank you."

I was so shocked that I could hardly believe my ears. Before I could get a grip on myself, Nina was calling for someone else to come in. I sort of stumbled out into the street only to discover that I couldn't remember where I'd parked my car. It was just one of those days. Interestingly, though, today Nina will take only people who are between five nine and five eleven. I knew better than to take the rejection personally, but no matter how long you're in the business, it's very hard not to. From that day on, I've been five seven.

I didn't give up. I went down my checklist of modeling agents and next on my list was Bill Cunningham, a respected and successful agent with an office in Beverly Hills. I was sitting in his waiting room when he happened to walk through and notice me. "Who is that girl?" he asked the receptionist. He agreed to represent me, and my career as a model in Hollywood took off. I got work almost immediately, modeling for newspaper ads and catalog layouts for Bullock's, one of Los Angeles's largest department stores.

Then I signed with a commercial agency, Sutton, Barth, and Vennari, and started going on interviews for commercials for such companies as Tide, Avon, Toyota, and Kodak. One of the toughest parts of going out on these interviews is to enter a waiting room that is filled with twenty or even thirty other women, each of whom is at least ten times more beautiful than you. No matter how good you look or how good you feel about yourself, one up-close glance at the competition can be devastating. Whenever I'd start to feel like I wanted to turn around and go back home, I'd remember something that Momma used to say: "If you can't stand the heat, get out of the kitchen." But who knew that the kitchen would be standing room only?

After a week of rejection, I'd go home and ask myself if it was all worth it. Then I'd cry countless tears of frustration, feeling like I was no good. I asked myself the same questions a million times: "Who am I fooling?" "What's wrong with me?" "Why did I choose this business?" "Why don't I just go into real estate or become a nurse?" Of course, I never really had an answer. I don't know why exactly, but I still felt that I could make it. I wasn't sure how or when, but I just believed that I could. And then I'd remember what Momma told me and vow that I'd never do something I would regret, like giving up.

Still, that did little to alleviate my depression about things.

I went home in the spring and was happy to see that Momma was still doing great. We had a wonderful time and her continued good health seemed like a miracle. In L.A. I'd call her whenever I had a few extra dollars or a few moments, just to hear her voice. Or I'd write to her. I sent her letters several times a week. If I was on an assignment out of town, I'd scribble out a quick note on hotel stationery or a postcard. Since I'd left home, my relationship with Momma had changed. We were somehow closer. While I was living in Atlanta, she would come to visit and we'd go out, more like girlfriends instead of mother and daughter. She also confided in me more.

But as close as we were, I knew that Momma always held things in. Where another person might scream about something, she'd keep it to herself. Daddy was somewhat the same, and as a result, our family, while very loving, was not really demonstrative or expressive. Plus, Momma worried a lot about everything. I know she did that because she loved us, but I could never see where this incessant worrying ever helped anything, and I vowed that I'd never become a constant worrier. It just seemed to do more harm than good. I've always believed that Momma's holding things in contributed to her getting cancer.

Though things were going great for her, they took a turn for the worse in April. She started losing weight rapidly, and her energy level was so low that she could barely drag herself from bed to go to work. Our family doctor insisted that Daddy take her back to the Medical University of South Carolina in Charleston, where she'd had her lung operation about eleven months earlier. Before she left to have more tests, I wrote to her: "Don't let the trip to Charleston get you down. I know how strong and confident you are and that's all it takes. If you do have surgery, just think what you will have to look forward to after you recuperate. First, you'll have a clean bill of health, then you'll be coming to L.A. to help me with my career. You know I can't make it without you!" Re-reading that letter as I write this book reminds me of how hopeful we all were then.

The first and most important test she underwent was a CAT scan, an advanced computerized X ray–type technique that can pinpoint internal tumors and irregularities without surgery. The scan is very noisy and time-consuming. Daddy was with her, and when it was all over, she felt so weak that she fell asleep in the waiting room with her head on his shoulder. The doctors there told them that there was no hope, that Momma had only a short time to live. Additional surgery would be futile, but they did advise Momma to start radiation and chemotherapy treatments as a way to slow the cancer's progress enough that she could be more comfortable. She left the doctor's office crying.

Despite her condition, Momma insisted on staying

in her own apartment. She zealously guarded her independence, and though Daddy wanted her to move back so he could take better care of her, she refused. Daddy would go back and forth from the post office or home to Momma's apartment to give her her medication. She also had her friends, Peggy Hursey, Polly Lowman, Mike Little, Libby Owens, and Uncle Bob, a man in his eighties who, though not a blood relative, had always loved Momma like she was his own daughter. They all stopped by regularly to spend time with her. Libby later told me that Momma talked about dying, and that she was angry about not being able to do the things she wanted to do. Momma made her friends swear that they wouldn't call me in California and tell me how bad off she was. Momma would say, "Vanna's trying to get her career off the ground, and that's more important right now." Momma would muster all her strength and then call me in Los Angeles. She sounded tired but spirited. I never had a clue that she might be dying.

On Tuesday, May 13, 1980, she wrote in her make-shift diary: "Today began the first day of a new life for me. I'm really lucky as I can plan from now on . . . as the end is forthcoming. I have many good friends that need to be told. It was a heavy day as I have already told Chip; still have to tell Vanna. Felt real bad about lying to her last night, but the time just wasn't right. God knows, I love my children."

The loose pages of this diary, which I found among

Momma's possessions after she died, kept careful account of her progress for the next nine days. She noted on that first day that she weighed 104 pounds; she would die six weeks later weighing only 68, no more than a child.

Typically, though, Momma worried about everyone else. Of Chip, who was then nineteen, she wrote: "God love him and look out for him. He is still young." On May 15, she wrote: "Vanna called. I can't quite get it under control with her yet. . . . Hope time continues to go slow for me. I have so many decisions to make (God help me make them correctly). I don't want to mess up everyone's lives, as I will soon be gone and their lives will continue on."

Daddy slept on the living room sofa at Momma's apartment, just in case something happened. He was dating a woman at the time, and Momma even worried about that: "I know it is hard on her to share him even under these circumstances," she noted, her script becoming lighter and less well formed with each passing day.

Over Memorial Day weekend, Daddy phoned me. He sounded very upset. "Vanna honey, can you come home? Your Momma needs you." I knew something was terribly wrong, and I was afraid to think what. Deep down, though, I knew. I told Daddy I'd be there the next day. He met me in Charleston, and during the two-hour drive to North Myrtle Beach, he tried to prepare me for the worst. I heard every word he said, but somehow I didn't believe him until

I saw her. She had lost so much weight since I'd last seen her only weeks earlier. She was a small woman to begin with—just five foot three—but she was already down to ninety pounds. I had a huge lump in my throat when I saw her sitting on a chair in the living room. It took all my strength not to break down in front of her. I knew then why I had come home. Still, though, Momma tried to act as if nothing were wrong. For the first time in her life, she just couldn't bring herself to tell me the truth.

I moved into Momma's apartment and the two of us slept together in her king-size bed. For the next five weeks, I thought of nothing but her. At night I dreamed about her; during the day I worried about her. She would always put on this brave front, telling me that she was fine and insisting that I go back to California and continue my career. Whenever she'd say something about my career, I'd think of how much it meant to her. Here I was doing something she'd always wanted to do, but in reality my career was so insignificant, so unimportant compared with something like this. It was all I could do to keep from crying whenever she'd start talking about how she was keeping me from making it big. The irony is that Momma is the reason why I made it big.

Being home to celebrate Momma's forty-fourth birthday on June 2 was really special. Coincidentally I was on television that morning as a contestant on *The Price Is Right*. A few weeks earlier I'd gone with a girlfriend named Brenda Moore to see a taping.

While we were standing in line, some of the show's staff asked some of us questions. This is how they choose who will get to "come on down." I was dressed very casually that day in a skintight T-shirt with the saying "Get Serious" on it. We were seated in the audience when Johnny Olson called out, "Vanna White, come on down!" I couldn't believe my ears. I looked over at Brenda, jumped up and down, then ran down the aisle to my position by the stage. This was my big chance to get rich—and be seen on national television. I was so nervous I could barely speak, much less think of prices, so I kept looking in the monitor at Brenda's face; I needed her ideas on how much to bid. Finally Bob Barker embarrassed me by saying—on national television—"Vanna, if you would quit looking at yourself in the monitor, you might win something!"

I'll never forget watching the show with Momma that day and the expression on her face when she saw me. She looked so happy and proud. She was absolutely thrilled. I don't think she would have been happier if I'd won an Academy Award. As it turned out, all I "won" were some lovely parting gifts.

Soon after Momma's birthday, things went downhill rapidly. The radiation treatments and chemotherapy made her deathly ill. She started to lose her appetite, and I had to force her to eat. All she wanted was cantaloupe. Sometimes she would crave fried chicken and one of her friends would stop by Floyd's Restaurant (where I'd worked as a teenager) and pick up some. They'd drop whatever they were doing and rush it over, but once the food arrived, Momma would just stare at it.

She got weaker and thinner as the pain grew more intense. I forced her to take the pain pills the doctor had prescribed. She was opposed to medicine in principle, but she needed to rest. Her friends would stop by to relieve me. Peggy would bring homemade custard, which Momma loved. Still, Momma was losing more than a pound a day. Finally accepting the futility of it all, we stopped the radiation and chemotherapy treatments. By this point, Momma barely had the strength to walk even a few steps. Toward the end, I had to literally carry her everywhere she wanted to go in the house, even if it was only to the bathroom.

Around this time we heard that some of the townspeople were putting together a big benefit for Momma. Poopoo McLaughlin and J. O. Baldwin, who owned part of the Holiday Inn where Momma had worked, started collecting money to help defray some of the medical costs. When Momma heard about it, she was somewhat embarrassed, but was so touched by everyone's concern that she wanted to be there. Unfortunately, she was too ill to attend the Joan White Benefit on June 4 at the Holiday Inn—North. Chip and I accepted a check for ten thousand dollars in front of a cheering crowd, and there wasn't a dry eye in the house. It was quite a tribute to Momma, and it was nice to know that everyone realized and appreciated all she had done for the town. I thought of how hard Momma had worked on behalf of the Heart Fund. Every February she would take over the airwaves of station WNMB for three consecutive days without sleep and raise money for the organization. She was known as the "Queen of Hearts."

After the benefit I wrote a letter of thanks that ran in the *North Myrtle Beach Times*. It read, in part: ". . . It showed that there are still people left in this world with real hearts full of true friendship and love. Although Mother was unable to attend, she told me how she felt and wanted me to express it to you. So on my mother's behalf, we thank you again, North Myrtle Beach, for everything."

The next few weeks were nothing short of hell. Momma's pain was horrendous; even the medication she did take didn't seem to help that much. Peggy would come by the apartment anytime she was in the area, occasionally even leaving real-estate clients in the backseat of her car while she popped in to see if we needed anything. One night Momma took Peggy's hand, then mine, and put them together. "Promise you'll take care of my little girl when I die, Peggy." She and Peggy were close, and Peggy is like part of the family to me. Once when I wasn't in the room, she told Peggy that she wanted to be cremated and have her ashes scattered over the ocean she loved so much. One day in early July, Reverend Marion Crooks stopped by to see Momma. She pulled him closer to her and said the words I never thought I'd hear her say: "I'm finished."

That night, while we were sleeping in her bed, Momma started having a seizure. It was one in the morning and when I realized what was happening, it frightened me so that I didn't know what to do. I ran down to Shirley Skinner's apartment, two doors away, told her what was happening and she came running. I felt so inadequate to help my mother. The paramedics arrived within minutes. That particular seizure ended, and Momma was lying there on the stretcher in a coma. For the first time, I really broke down. I couldn't believe that was my mother, lying there strapped down, just staring into space. I'll never forget the sound of the siren as it rushed Momma and me to the Grand Strand Hospital. The whole way there, I held her hand and kept telling her over and over that everything was going to be all right. She did not want to die in a hospital; she had told me so the day before. But what could I do? Deep down, we both knew that if she went into the hospital, she would never come home again. Still, it was impossible to witness her seizure and believe that keeping her at home was the right thing to do.

The next morning the doctor confirmed that the cancer had spread to her brain, and that it was only a matter of days before the end. She had seizure after seizure, and with each one she regressed deeper into childhood. Although the prospect of that happening frightens many people, it actually proved to be something of a blessing, for in those last few days, she was happier and more content than I'd ever seen her. She actually seemed to be getting better. She was sitting up in bed, pretending to drink something through an imaginary straw. I asked, "Momma, what are you drinking?" and she replied with a contented, childlike expression on her face, "A chocolate milk-shake!" That entire day was all fun and smiles and laughs. She really was a little kid again. Daddy and Chip were there as often as they could be, and they made her laugh. At one point she got out of bed and wanted to look out the window. Even though we knew that she was just delirious, seeing her like this was much better than watching her writhe in pain.

Late that night while I was sitting at the edge of her hospital bed, she leaned over to me, squeezed my cheeks with both hands, gave me a big kiss on the lips, and said, "Vanna darling, I love you." Peggy was there that night too, and we watched Momma maintain this incredible level of energy. She refused to go to sleep. I think she realized that if she did, she would never awaken. That morning, the doctor couldn't believe that she had not slept at all. He had been giving her lots of medication to sleep and for the pain. He told me that if she wasn't sleepy by nightfall, then he would have to increase the dosage; he warned me that it might prove fatal. The day went on, with Momma still as giddy as a teenager. She hadn't slept in nearly two days. At eight o'clock the doctor came by, and noticing that her vital signs were weakening, he increased the dosage. Although it was clear that the end was imminent and that Momma might not survive, I told the doctor to do what he thought was best for her.

When she finally did doze off at about ten that night, I went back to her apartment to take a shower and get some rest. Since she'd had that first seizure, I'd been by her side day and night, getting what little sleep I could sitting up in a chair at her bedside. Once I got back to her apartment, all I could do was sit on the couch and stare into space. When I couldn't fall asleep, I went back to the hospital. At two-thirty in the morning I was there with Peggy and our minister. Momma was sleeping peacefully, her eyes almost but not quite shut. I sat by her bedside, rubbing her hands and telling her how much I loved her. She didn't have the strength to respond, but tears started streaming down her cheeks. I held on to her hand tightly and thought I saw her trying to smile at me. A second later, she started gasping for air; two minutes later she was gone.

The instant that I realized she was dead, I stood up and felt a warm spirit streaking through my body. I became hysterical, then buried my face into Peggy's chest. I guess all that I had been holding in for so long just had to come out, and it did. But once that happened, I sensed a feeling of peace and comfort. I knew that Momma's suffering was over forever, and that she would always be with me.

The day before Momma died Peggy and I had made arrangements for the cremation. Momma had wanted to donate her organs, but there was just too much cancer. The day after Momma's death, there was a quiet memorial service for her at Trinity Methodist Church. It was standing room only. Reverend Crooks began his eulogy and everyone broke down. Peggy had to get up and go to the back of the church. Daddy, Chip, and I tried to be strong, but it wasn't easy. When the service ended, the three of us thanked everyone who had come. I always remember that the birds all seemed to be singing so much louder than usual that morning.

The funeral home delivered Momma's ashes in a small box to Peggy, who had arranged with North Myrtle Beach Mayor Joe Saleeby to take them up in his small plane and scatter them along the shoreline. I couldn't bring myself to witness that, but Chip stood on the shore and watched. We spent the next couple days going through Momma's things, sorting out forty-four years of her life. I kept her diary, some of her clothes, and her wedding ring.

With everything taken care of, I returned to California three days later. A week or so after that, I was in a department store dressing room, trying on clothes. Through the partition I heard a daughter and her mother discussing how various items of clothing looked—just the same way Momma and I would talk. I sat down on the little bench in my cubicle and cried my eyes out for ten minutes. I missed Momma so much. I always will.

I came back to Hollywood from North Myrtle Beach that summer with more determination than ever. Momma taught me that if you have a goal and work hard enough and don't let anything get in your way, you can make it. Although that may sound a bit simplistic, I believe it. I had learned from my mother's example that it could happen, and no matter how many rejections I got, I wasn't going to just give up.

As soon as I'd gotten back, I immediately started getting modeling assignments, but I really wanted to do movies or television. I made a lot of mistakes when I started going out on auditions for TV spots, such as wearing too much makeup, or dressing too glamorously. It took me a little while to realize that agencies and clients who make commercials want their actors to look like the average, everyday person who uses Tide or Doublemint Gum. Of course, there's no school that can teach you this. You have to depend on the advice of others, preferably your personal manager.

A personal manager is not an agent; the agent is a person who is constantly, actively looking for work for you. Ideally, an agent knows enough people, and is well enough known to everyone else in the business, that he knows what's going on and who is looking for what. When he hears about something you might be good in—commercial, movie, whatever— it is his job to call the producers or whoever is responsible for the upcoming audition and submit you for the part. In exchange for these services, the agent is paid a commission based on a percentage (usually ten percent) of your earnings. California state law requires that agents be licensed. Though there probably are some unscrupulous agents, the state's regulatory laws surely weed out some of the worst.

Managers are another matter. The manager is an adviser who helps ensure that you get the best deal possible, with terms and conditions that are compatible with your long-range career goals. A good manager helps you to decide which jobs are good to take and which are not. If you're really lucky, your manager is like a supportive friend with a mind of his own. When issues come up that need to be discussed, he can play devil's advocate and help you to see all the angles. He can also handle many details of your business, so you can concentrate on your work. A good manager is a godsend. Now that I have a truly great manager, Ray Manzella, I know what it takes. When I first came to Hollywood, however, it was a different matter.

I didn't know where to start looking for a personal manager, so a close friend introduced me to his, a guy I'll call Tom (not his real name). I met Tom at an art auction held at the Hollywood Palladium on Sunset Boulevard. I also met several performers there whom I'd seen on television, comedian Marty Allen, Lorne Greene, and Dick York, among others. When I talked with Tom, I learned that he had quite a number of well-known clients. He seemed to be impressed with me despite the fact that I had no credits or any real television or movie experience. After thinking it over with the little information I had, I signed a three-year contract with him. It was his job to introduce me to the right people and he did. Through Tom I got an agent named Ron Mason. I also met Judy Schade, who ran a modeling agency in Century City. She sent me out on interviews for various modeling assignments, then one day she phoned and told me to call the offices of Lynn Stalmaster, a well-known casting agent, who was rounding up talent for a movie called *Looker*.

The movie's screenwriter and director, Michael

Crichton, described the film as "a thriller about television commercials." And I guess that just about summed it up. The film starred James Coburn as the head of a giant conglomerate whose experiments in mind control through TV commercials set off a chain of bizarre murders, and Albert Finney, in his Hollywood film debut, as Dr. Larry Roberts, a Beverly Hills plastic surgeon. Interestingly, the female lead was played by Susan Dey, who as Laurie Partridge in the old *Partridge Family* television series, had been one of my role models when I was a kid.

Needless to say, I was thrilled to be cast as one of the models, known as the Reston girls, even though I did not have any lines. The shooting, which was to begin in October, was delayed due to the actors' strike. My first day on the set was November 18 and I was so excited I could hardly stand it. I wrote in my diary that night: "It's like a dream come true." And it really was. We filmed one scene on a beach north of Malibu as if it were summer. We were all in skimpy bathing suits, playing volleyball, and acting as if it were sweltering outside when, in fact, it was quite cold. My other scenes, all with Albert Finney, wound up on the proverbial cutting-room floor, but that was okay. It was just great to finally have made it into a movie, even with as small a part as mine. I worked on the film for two weeks. Later, when the film came out, I was on the screen for only about twenty seconds. Despite that, I was very excited, though the movie was not a big hit.

Within a few days of completing my work on my first movie, I got another movie part, this one for a film called *Graduation Day*. It was a thriller about a slasher who preys on high school students. Uncle Chris was the male lead, as the coach of Midvale High, and I was a cheerleader. I had four or five scenes, including the "high drama" scene where I discover a dead body in my locker and let loose a blood-curdling scream (I did it in one take!). It was a low-budget horror flick, but the experience wasn't a total loss. Because I'd had some lines, I qualified for my Screen Actors' Guild card. And, even better, when the movie came out, the Ocean Cinema in North Myrtle Beach, South Carolina, held a big premiere in my honor. It was exciting to see my name up in lights on the marquee, as if I were the star! In fact, the headline in the local paper read, "Movie Star Returns to North Myrtle Beach." It was a very nice gesture and I was quite proud. Lots of my friends were there, including Mayor Saleeby, who presented me with a bouquet of red roses. He also asked me for a life-size picture of myself to use against the local citizens who were complaining about the town's drinking water. He wanted to be able to point to my picture and say, "Look at what drinking Myrtle Beach water did for her!"

And *then* I got yet another part! That was three in a row. This time it was in a two-hour made-for-TV thriller called *The Burning*, starring Melissa Sue Anderson, Marion Ross, and my friend Patrick Cassidy. I played a cheerleader named DeVona and had only a few lines, but that didn't really matter. Three film parts, just like that! I felt very lucky. When the movie finally aired six weeks later on ABC, it was retitled *Midnight Offerings*. From the way things were going, it would seem that Tom was really doing a great job.

In early 1981 I moved from Oakwood to an apartment of my own on Camino Palmero. Without a roommate I was now totally responsible for the rent, so that did put the pressure on, career-wise. But I really had no reason to think that things weren't going to keep going this great for a long time to come. It was a nice one-bedroom and loft apartment, just across the street from where Sylvester Stallone had lived before he made it, and just one block south of the house where Ozzie and Harriet used to live. I felt like this might be a lucky location. I could only hope.

Though I'd been in Los Angeles just a little over a year, I was slowly—and in some cases, painfully—learning how Hollywood really worked. It all came to a head at the birthday party Tom threw for me in February. Of course, I was very happy about the party, but there was something dishonest about it. In the two-page ad Tom took out in *Variety*, the show-biz daily, he alluded to two forthcoming films that I was supposed to be in that never came to anything (in fact, as I found out later, I was never even signed to do them). That was bad enough. The real kicker was that he insisted that I say I was turning twenty-one, not twenty-four. At that time, I believed that the films were in the works, so I rationalized that there was no harm in lying about my age. I looked twenty-one, and I was convinced that everyone else in Hollywood lied about their ages and that everyone in the industry expected it. Things were going so well with Tom, I didn't speak up against it. It just didn't seem to be that big a deal. Besides, I thought he was a good manager.

The birthday party was nice, but it was a bit of an embarrassment. About one hundred fifty people showed up, including Peter Lawford, Mike Connors, Lyle Waggoner, Jack Klugman, Karen Black, Christopher George, Lynda Day George, many casting directors, and a few producers. I didn't really know these people; it had all been arranged. And though I was thrilled to meet some of these stars, it still didn't feel right to me.

It all hit me when I met a fellow South Carolinian named Bo Hopkins. He was also trying to make it in Hollywood. He told me that it was nice to meet a southern girl who had not gone Hollywood, who remembered her roots and could act like a real lady. I was flattered. At the same time, though, his comments just seemed to drive home how far from that I was beginning to stray. I was raised to be forthright, honest, and never to lie. And letting a manager lie for me wasn't that much different from me doing the lying myself. It took a while, but I finally made the move and left my first manager.

I'm not sure whether it was related to leaving Tom or not, but the work did drop off a little bit. More than once I faced a serious cash crunch, and I would take an occasional job waitressing to make ends meet. At one point, I was really strapped for cash. The rent was due, and I was desperate. I knew that I should have called Daddy and asked for a short-term loan. I know that he would have gladly loaned me the money, but I just couldn't bring myself to do it.

I so wanted Daddy to think that everything was okay that I did something that I've regretted ever since. I was offered a job modeling lingerie for an ad. This wasn't the kind of basic bras-and-panties stuff you'd see in the Spiegel catalog. It was sexier lingerie, sheerer and more revealing, and available only through mail order. At the time I was a little surprised at how risqué the pieces were, but today I see things just as revealing in department stores. I was contacted and offered a lot of money, more money than I'd made on any one job since I'd come to L.A. Although I should have known better, I could see only one solution to my problem—do the shoot, get the money, pay the rent, and avoid eviction.

I made an appointment to do the shoot. The photographer came to my apartment, and a few hours later the shoot was done. Usually models do not shoot at their own homes, but I told the photographer that I would feel much more comfortable doing it there, and he agreed to come over. There was nothing strange about the shoot, but from the moment I accepted the job and every day since, I've regretted it. Revealing my body like that was uncomfortable for me, and it upset me that I was doing something like that for money. Still, even with doing it in my home, the whole thing felt wrong, and I hated it. The more I thought about it, the more I had to face the fact that I'd made a mistake. I knew I was doing the wrong thing, but I wouldn't know just how wrong it was until over five years later. The last part of the story comes later, but I learned an excellent lesson, one that no one should have to learn: Never, ever do something you feel uncomfortable about—no matter what the reason. I guarantee you, it will come back to haunt you.

By mid-1981 I decided that I needed a change in my commercial agent. Despite the film work I had gotten, nothing was happening for me in commercials. I had been on over one hundred interviews and not gotten a single job. So I changed agents. Now, most times, changing agents is not the answer, but in this case it was. Dean Parker, vice president at Abrams-Rubaloff & Lawrence, agreed to take me on. One of the first interviews I was sent on was for a Miller Beer spot.

I'd gone on so many interviews that this was just

another. But the trick to succeeding in this field is to approach each interview enthusiastically, no matter how many rejections you've got behind you.

Generally, the first interview is for a look. All I have to do is look into a video camera and say, "Hi, I'm Vanna White. Abrams-Rubaloff." That's it. If they like you, they'll call you back within two or three days. The casting people have called your agent in the meantime and told him that they are interested in seeing you again.

And they were—I got an appointment to see them again. The second time you may be asked to say something different. Everybody approaches the callback, as it's called, differently, but I always wear the same outfit I wore on the first interview. Again, it's an on-camera audition. "Hi, I'm Vanna White. Abrams-Rubaloff." But this time a casting person may ask, "Vanna, what do you plan to do for the rest of the day?" It's not that he or she really cares, but when you answer this simple question, the casting person will be looking at how you speak, how you sound, how you move, what you do with your hands, and so on. For this Miller Beer interview I said, "I have a gynecologist's appointment . . . but you can't come!" The guy laughed, and perhaps that gave him something to remember me by. (In fact, though, I really did have a doctor's appointment.) Usually, there are several more such callbacks for the same commercial, but this time I got the word the next day that the job was mine.

Seven of us—men and women—flew up to Seattle, Washington, and sat around a country-and-western bar, drinking beer and laughing while a band played. Of course, we couldn't be shown in the commercial actually drinking the beer, but we did drink between takes. Sounds like fun, huh? The best part was yet to come. This was my first national spot, and though the fee for the actual shooting was just a few hundred dollars plus the travel costs, the real payoff was in residuals, the fee you get each and every time the commercial airs. As you probably know, there's always a beer commercial airing somewhere, and over the next year I made about fifteen thousand dollars in residuals.

The movie jobs had dried up, so I was depending more on modeling jobs again. For a few months that spring I took a job that my friend had told me about, working with two game-show producers who were developing a new show called *Pot of Gold*. I've always loved game shows. In fact, when I was living in Atlanta, I watched *Wheel of Fortune* every morning that I didn't have a modeling assignment. I even wrote to the show and asked if I could get on it as a contestant. I got back the usual form letter saying that I could come out and auditon, if I paid all my expenses out to Los Angeles. There went that idea.

Working on *Pot of Gold* was a lot of fun; it was interesting to see how a show was put together from scratch. One part of my job was playing the game over and over and over again; that's the only way you can be sure that all the "bugs" are worked out before it goes on the air. In June 1981 we went over to the NBC studio in Burbank (where I work now, coincidentally) and did a major run-through for the network. We all had high hopes that the show would take off, but, like most other pilots and ideas, it never got on the air.

It was back to the usual routine of trying to get work. But over the years I'd learned that things can turn out all right when you least expect it. One month I was facing the rent coming due with no idea of how I was going to pay it. Just then I got a job to model at a program the Big Brothers of America was holding to thank the major corporations who'd donated substantial sums to them. Each model acted as a "cheerleader" for a particular company (I was assigned to Carnation), and we rooted for that company as it competed for a brand-new Cadillac. My company won the car! I had fun that day, collected my little fee, went home, and resumed worrying about the rent. A few days later I went to the mailbox and found an envelope from Carnation. Inside was a "bonus" check equal to more than my rent. It seems that whenever I hit what feels like rock bottom, a miracle occurs.

I was starting to feel lucky, and I believe that also played a part in my meeting the love of my life, John Gibson. One afternoon in 1979, when I was living in Atlanta, I caught *The Merv Griffin Show*. Usually I never watched daytime TV—I was always too busy

—but this day I happened to be in bed with the flu. There I saw John Gibson, a dancer at Chippendale's, a new nightclub where the guys stripped down to their G-strings for the ladies, being interviewed. The Chippendale's phenomenon has since spread to all parts of the country, but back then it was all the rage only in Los Angeles. I thought John looked great, and as soon as he opened his mouth, I thought to myself, this guy is a real person. He was genuine, down-to-earth, and seemed to have a great sense of humor. Something just clicked inside my head, and I knew that I had to meet him someday.

Shortly after I had settled in Los Angeles, I went to Chippendale's, hoping to meet John. The first time I went, he was there, and I introduced myself. We talked, and I was flirting with him pretty heavily; then a few hours later John said that he already had a girlfriend. I was disappointed, but I asked him if it would be all right for us to be friends, and he said yes. After that, I would go to the nightclub now and then with some friends, and say hello to him after the show. This went on for a year. Finally, on December 3, 1981, a friend told me that John and his girlfriend had broken up. I made up my mind to attract his attention, and the next day—December 4— we were together. We had a few drinks and talked for hours. He was wonderful to be with—warm, caring, witty, bright, and very much the gentleman. He was everything I'd ever wanted.

The next Saturday we had our first real date. John

took me to a Christmas party aboard a yacht that was moored at Marina del Rey. For Christmas the owners of all the boats decorated them with strings of colored lights and ornaments. It turned out to be a romantic evening, and I felt myself falling madly in love with John. From this point on, John and I were nearly inseparable. As we spent more time together and I got to know John even better, I was happy to find out that all my first impressions were confirmed. He was as good as he seemed the first time I saw him. John was a product of Middle America, born in Grayling, Michigan, on July 15, 1948, to Neva and Leo Gibson. When I met him, of course, he was handsome, well-built—simply a great-looking guy. But once when John showed me some pictures of himself, taken back when he was studying for his B.A. in business administration at the University of Michigan, I couldn't believe my eyes. I didn't even recognize him. In an interview he described himself like this: "I was overweight, wore glasses, and had a big gap in my teeth." I guess that's as good a description as any.

Despite his own misgivings, John married his college sweetheart right out of school because it seemed like the thing to do. He went to work at his father's Detroit used-car dealership and was miserable. One day, just thirteen months after his wedding, he wrote his wife a long letter and left for Aspen, Colorado.

Going to Aspen was a turning point for John. He was only twenty-three and ready to make changes in his life. He worked tending bar and taught skiing. He also started taking better care of his body by working out.

Having tired of the "make-believe" atmosphere in Aspen, John moved to West Palm Beach, Florida, where he took up carpentry, something he enjoyed doing all his life. He also kept working on himself. He traded his glasses for contact lenses, had his teeth capped, and started taking voice lessons. I guess that he had seen how a change in his looks was changing his life. But that was only the beginning.

In late 1974 his girlfriend submitted Polaroids of John in the nude to *Playgirl* magazine. The editors liked what they saw and invited John out to L.A. for a photo session. His nude layout—including a centerfold—ran in the April 1975 issue. It literally changed John's life. He moved to California, and began working as a model and studying acting. He appeared in print ads in newspapers and magazines, and on billboards. He tended bar at night to pay for his acting lessons, and ironically, he got his first acting break when a producer of *General Hospital* saw him tending bar at a function he attended. John then played a bartender in six separate episodes of the daytime soap.

But the real turning point came when John became a "male exotic dancer" at a new Culver City, California, club called Chippendale's. Though John described his role as a "male stripper," he didn't remove all of his clothing. Like just about everything that John did, that one thing soon led to another. The casting people from *The Young and the Restless,* another daytime soap, saw John on Merv's show, liked his style and look, and suggested to the producer and writers that they create a character for him. That character was Jerry "Cash" Cashman, a slick hustler who was also an exotic dancer at Bayou's, a nightclub set in the series' fictional city. Though Cash was originally intended to appear in only five shows, John was an instant hit with viewers. He stayed on the show for almost a year and a half.

John had no problem holding down the two jobs —filming the soap and working at Chippendale's. He once described Chippendale's as "more play than anything else," and he told me several times that performing in front of women made him feel "terrific." John saw the Chippendale's job as a stepping stone, and he made great money there. I didn't really like the idea of him dancing at Chippendale's but I would never ask him to quit. Also, in the beginning, he stayed out after work until very late. After our relationship developed, he was usually home around eleven.

After about sixteen months John left *The Young and the Restless* when they killed off his character. I remember watching the last show with John and crying like a baby when Cash died. I knew it wasn't real, but I just couldn't stand the thought of John dying, even if he was only acting.

When we first met, John lived only about three

blocks from me, and within three months he had moved into my apartment. The first thing John had to contend with were my two cats, Rhett and Ashley. He had very strong allergic reactions to them, but he stuck it out, and he eventually got used to them. He also moved in his saltwater fish aquarium, and his two finches, Chip and Dale. We were all one big happy family until about a year later, when Rhett and Ashley had Chip and Dale for dinner.

During our first few months of living together in 1982, not much was really happening for either of us. John kept taking acting classes, going on job interviews, and working at Chippendale's. I was doing the standard interviews, auditions, and the occasional job. Since John and I were in the same business, we each understood what the other was going through, and that's always a big help. You never really get used to rejection, and you do need all the good, loving support you can get. It was really nice to be able to come home and share whatever had happened that day—good or bad—with someone who could sympathize.

Though things weren't going so great for us career-wise, we had a wonderful relationship. We both enjoyed hockey, polo, pool, and fishing. When John and I would visit his parents in Michigan, where they lived on a lake, we'd spend hours out fishing alone, just the two of us. We were also competitive, but in a nice way. I always caught the bigger fish. But I couldn't even begin to compete with him when it came to water and snow skiing. John was great at those sports, and my first attempts were pretty pathetic. Still, we had lots of fun, and that's what really mattered.

On Memorial Day weekend, 1982, I was in Palm Springs on a modeling assignment. That summer I was set to appear in an episode of a sitcom called *Star of the Family*, but that was just a one-shot and would only cover a couple months' rent. I'd also auditioned for *Star Search* in the "spokesmodel" category and got turned down. And at one point I even toyed with the idea of posing for *Playboy*. John had been a friend of Hugh Hefner's, and we often attended parties at the Playboy mansion. The idea was presented to me, John and I discussed it briefly, and I decided that I still couldn't pose nude like that, no matter how much it was worth. Being sexy is one thing; being naked is something else. Maybe I'm just old-fashioned, but that's how I've always felt.

On a whim I decided to visit a psychic in Palm Springs. She gave me a fairly long reading and told me many things about my life that she couldn't have possibly known except psychically. During the reading, she said, "In November you will sign a long-term television contract. You will sign with a man whose last name is Schwartz." Then she had a little trouble figuring out the first name, finally settling on McCoy. "I think it's McCoy Schwartz." While I thought the whole experience was interesting and reassuring, I had to laugh at the idea of getting a long-term television contract. I mean, it sounded great, but what were the odds that it was going to happen? I just kept it in the back of my mind when I returned to Los Angeles. At that time, I didn't know anyone by the name of Schwartz.

In September a friend called me to say that Susan Stafford, the hostess on *Wheel of Fortune*, was leaving the show and that I should try out for the job. I called my agent and asked him to submit me for consideration, and he promised to look into it. Moments later he called to tell me that Susan's replacement had already been chosen. Oddly enough, I had not been submitted for the job earlier because my agent had run out of 8×10 glossies of me.

Coincidentally, a few days later John and I went to the studio where another Merv Griffin show, *Dance Fever*, taped. Our friend Janet Jones was one of the dancers, and we met her there. I was dressed kind of wild, in skintight Spandex pants and spike-heeled boots. When Janet introduced me to Bob Murphy and Murray Schwartz of the Griffin organization, I asked them about the *Wheel* job and they said that they really hadn't made a final decision and that I should call them in early October. They gave me their business cards, and I made a note to myself to call. I didn't think that they'd see me again or even consider me for the job because of the crazy way I was dressed that day. Still, I had nothing to lose, so

I called. I was told that they still had not made a decision and that I should come down to their office to audition.

This time I dressed conservatively, a silk blouse and slacks. I met the show's producer, Nancy Jones, who interviewed me for about half an hour. I also met some other people who worked for the show. A week or so later they called me and told me to appear at the NBC studios in Burbank to do a brief on-camera audition with the show's host, Pat Sajak. There were about fifteen other girls there, and we each taped these short scenes on the *Wheel of Fortune* set. That was kind of exciting for me, having been a fan of the show for so long. But as it turned out, being a fan helped me too. I knew what Susan Stafford did and how to do it.

After this audition, they narrowed the field down a bit. The tapes had been sent over to the Griffin offices, where Nancy Jones, Murray Schwartz, Merv Griffin, and several other key people watched them, eliminating women as they viewed the tapes. Finally it got down to two: Vicki McCarty, a blue-eyed brunette and a friend of mine, and me. What really concerned me at this point was that Vicki spoke beautifully, while my experience talking on camera was so limited. The final decision would be made after Vicki and I each taped five real shows, to be aired nationally.

Vicki did hers first, then came my turn. I wasn't just nervous, I was beside myself. The shows would be aired on national television too. My nervousness really showed. My lower lip quivered; Pat Sajak even said that he could hear my knees knocking together. Afterward, Pat said to the staff, "Gee, she seems like a nice girl and she's obviously pretty, but you know she'll faint if she's out there." After the tapings, I was exhausted, physically and emotionally. I knew I'd been just awful, and that there was no chance of my getting this job. I figured that the Griffin people would call early the next morning and put me out of my misery by telling me point-blank that I'd blown it. But that's not what happened.

For two weeks I waited and waited. Every time the phone rang, I jumped. While my friends and John were all saying that I had nothing to worry about, that I had the job, I knew deep in my heart that I hadn't got the job. And with things going the way they had in the past few months, that meant that I might have to seriously reevaluate my career and my life. Maybe it was time to give up on show business. Maybe now was the time to get into real estate or go back to waitressing. I tried to rationalize things, to talk myself into believing that maybe being on television wasn't so great. But I knew in my heart that this was what I'd really wanted, what I'd worked so hard for. At the same time, though, I accepted that I probably wouldn't get it.

On November 24, Thanksgiving Eve, the phone rang.

"Hello," I answered.

"Hello, Vanna. This is Nancy Jones."

My heart was pounding so hard I could see my sweatshirt jump. "Hi," I said, trying my hardest to sound cheerful.

"Well, congratulations. You've got the job!"

I was stunned. I tried to be cool, but it was tough. I screamed, which sent Rhett and Ashley scooting under the bed, and my mind went blank. I hung up just as John was coming in the front door.

"Who was that on the phone?" he asked.

"Nancy Jones. You know, the producer of *Wheel*." I tried to look glum and disappointed.

"Oh, you didn't get it. I'm sorry, honey."

"I got it! I got it!" I shouted, leaping into his arms. It was like a scene out of an old movie. We hugged and kissed. We were so happy.

I called all my friends and family, then John and I went out for a great celebratory dinner, with champagne, of course. It was a wonderful evening.

I later learned that I was chosen because Merv thought I turned the letters better than anyone else and Nancy Jones thought that Pat and I made a "cute couple," with a sort of brother and sister look. Whatever. I was just glad I'd been chosen. A few days later I went in to sign my contract. It was long-term, it was television, and it was with Murray—not McCoy—Schwartz.

7

♥

But enough about just me, for now. Of course, if it weren't for *Wheel of Fortune*, I wouldn't be writing this book now. And I know from talking with hundreds of people every month that there's no end to the questions fans have about the show. So this chapter will be your crash course in everything you'd want to know about *Wheel of Fortune*, including some tips about how to get on it yourself.

Wheel of Fortune was created by Merv Griffin. When most people think of Merv, it's his famous talk show that comes to mind first. What many don't know is that Merv, with his former wife, Julann, created the game show *Jeopardy* back in the early sixties. Among

the other shows Merv developed were *Play Your Hunch,
One in a Million, Reach for the Stars, Let's Play Post
Office,* and *The Memory Game.*

Supposedly, Merv had loved to play Hangman when
he was a kid. When he got older and was touring
the country with the Freddy Martin Orchestra, he
played the game with the other musicians. According
to the legend, Merv one day began thinking about
playing Hangman and getting ideas about how to
turn that game's premise—guessing letters to solve
a word puzzle—into a game show. Even today, Merv
still submits puzzle ideas, sometimes scribbled on the
backs of napkins and pieces of scratch paper. It seems
that Merv, an avid crossword puzzle fan, has never
lost interest in word games of all types.

Of course, *Wheel of Fortune* probably wouldn't have
gotten on the air if it were just a televised Hangman
game. Several other elements were added, the main
one being the wheel. Three contestants each take
turns spinning a large (almost eight feet wide) wheel
that has sections, each of which signifies an amount
of money, loss of a turn, bankruptcy (where the player
loses all the money he's accumulated thus far in that
round), or some special prize that the contestant will
get if he solves the puzzle. A player may spin as long
as he continues to call out consonants or purchases
vowels (at $250 each) that are in the puzzle, or as
long as he has a free spin due him. Once a contestant
calls out a letter not on the board or runs out of free
spins, his turn is up and the next contestant spins.

The puzzle—which can be a person or fictional character or group of people, a thing, a title, an event, a phrase, an occupation, or a place—is up on the puzzle board with the letters obscured. All the contestants know about the puzzle is how many words are in the answer, how many letters are in each word, whether or not the answer contains any hyphens or apostrophes, and what category the answer falls under. The puzzle is solved when, during his turn, a contestant gives the correct answer.

Now, sometimes the puzzle can be solved with just a few letters revealed, and other times almost all the letters will have to be up before someone gets the answer. There are also lots of times when contestants know the answer, but decide to keep spinning the wheel in hopes of racking up more money with which to buy prizes. All the prize money is spent on prizes or credited to gift certificates at specific stores. We've added a cash jackpot round to the daytime show. It starts out at $1,000 and increases by a thousand dollars a day until someone wins it. Of course, a player could hit bankrupt at any time and lose all the money accumulated during that round. And that's where the gambling aspect of the game comes into play.

The contestant who solves the puzzle gets to buy prizes, which range from appliances, furniture, luggage, clothes, jewelry, shoes, artwork, rugs, recreational vehicles, cars, trips—just about everything you can imagine, including, of course, the show's unofficial mascot, the now famous ceramic dalmation (for

$154), whom I like to call Spot. Whoever has amassed the greatest amount of money and prizes at the end of the regular rounds, goes to the bonus round, where he solves another puzzle using only five consonants and one vowel of his choice in fifteen seconds or less. The bonus-round prize is usually a car, boat, dream vacation, or very generous gift certificate to a very upscale store, like a famous jeweler's, for example. I'm often asked why contestants in the bonus round sometimes choose to play for the dining room furniture instead of the car or other large prize on the set. According to the game's rules, a player can buy any prize on the floor at any time, if he has enough money. However, in the bonus round, he can select only from those prizes that have a large shiny gold star on them. For example, there may be a car on the floor, which could be bought at any time, but unless it has the star on it, it cannot be played for in the bonus round.

The show first aired on January 6, 1975, with host Chuck Woolery (who's since gone on to *Love Connection* and *Scrabble*) and Susan Stafford, an L.A.-based talk-show personality. At the time, hostesses were rare on game shows. According to our producer, Nancy Jones, it was Lin Bolen, the NBC vice president in charge of daytime programming, who first suggested expanding the hostess's role on *Wheel of Fortune*. Lin wanted the hostess to do more than just model and "tease" (that's what they call those graceful arm and hand gestures) the prizes. Though several women, including Betty White and Bess Myerson, had played significant roles on game shows, women were still in the minority compared to the number of male hosts on daytime television. Up until *Wheel* debuted, the most famous of the game-show women was *Let's Make a Deal*'s Carol Merrill, who was with that show from 1963 to when she left in 1977. During all those years, she spoke on camera only twice.

Lin's original idea was that *Wheel*'s hostess would not only turn the letters but also describe the prizes. That proved impossible because of the logistics of the game, so Susan continued turning the letters and saying "Bye-bye" at the end of each show.

Over the first seven years, the show held its own following but wasn't a huge across-the-boards hit. Three years after *Wheel* debuted, Chuck and Susan earned Emmy nominations for Outstanding Hosts of a Game Show. Around 1981, Chuck Woolery opted not to renew his contract, and the Griffin people launched the search for his replacement. There are several well-known game-show hosts they might have chosen for the spot, but they decided early on that they wanted a fresh face. They had to look no further than Los Angeles to find one.

Pat Sajak had come to Hollywood in March 1977 to work as weatherman on the local NBC affiliate. Previous to that he'd done five years as weatherman at Nashville station WSM, and before that had spent four years as a United States Army disc jockey stationed in Saigon during the Vietnam War. Even as a weatherman, Pat was very witty. He also hosted the NBC station's public-affairs program, *The Sunday Show*. There he honed his interviewing and ad-libbing skills, talking with a wide range of people, including various experts, politicians, authors, and others.

One of his fans was Merv Griffin, who later explained his choice of Pat to an interviewer like this: "I loved Pat's whimsical antics, and I thought he had the right characteristics for a game-show host, which is a guy who looks like your favorite son-in-law." In fact, two years before Chuck Woolery decided to leave the show, Merv had contacted Pat about another project. Pat had to decline then because of previous obligations. But when Pat was called about *Wheel of Fortune* in late 1981, right around his thirty-fifth birthday, he accepted it. *Wheel* was by then an established show, and though it wasn't yet the smash it would become a few years later, it was a network job, an important consideration for anyone working in broadcasting.

Pat debuted as host in December 1981, with Susan Stafford remaining as hostess. Part of Pat's appeal stems from the fact that he's become a great host by making a conscious effort not to become the stereotypical game-show host. Pat doesn't jump around, scream, shout, or kiss the contestants. He's just himself, a low-key, friendly guy with a terrific sense of humor and an incredible deadpan delivery. It seems that no target is sacred. Once, during a recent Christmas show, he informed the players that if they landed on bankrupt, they'd have to wear his maroon-colored jacket. Other times, he's kidded about the merchandise, or what I was wearing. It's all in good fun, and it's all so natural. He's just himself. And that helps put the players at ease, calms the audience and the rest of us down when technical problems arise and the taping's delayed, and makes for a great atmosphere to work in.

In late 1982, Susan Stafford left the show to move to Texas and work taking care of cancer patients. When I replaced Susan Stafford back in December 1982, we still had only the daytime version of the show. It was doing well enough, but things really went into high gear after the nighttime version debuted in syndication in September 1983. From then on, the number of viewers increased, and today *Wheel of Fortune* is seen by over forty-three million people a day. King World, the family-owned syndication company headed by brothers Michael and Roger King, has since seen its initial investment of $100,000 reap tens of millions in profits. The Kings also advised Murray Schwartz with some ideas about how to increase the nighttime version's appeal to viewers, by offering bigger money and more upscale prizes, like luxurious furs and fantasy dream vacations instead of the usual game-show staples like large household appliances. For example, while the daytime show's top-dollar on the wheel is $2,000 and the winning player returns the next day and may play up to three days in a row, nighttime contestants may appear on only one show, but the top-dollar on that wheel is higher, $5,000.

There are dozens of people working behind the scenes at *Wheel*, each performing a vital task. Nancy Jones, our producer, started in television as Chuck Barris's secretary but was quickly promoted to date coordinator of Barris's *The Dating Game*. She later worked as a script girl for Barris, then did production on various talk shows, sitcoms, and variety shows. In fall 1974 she went to work for Merv Griffin Enterprises, developing the pilot for *Wheel of Fortune*. After two months as associate producer, she became the show's producer.

Essentially, Nancy is the boss, after Merv, of course. She is on the set every day, overseeing the entire staff, meeting weekly with Merv Griffin to select the puzzles that will be used (he retains the final say on that), and selecting the prizes. She also helps screen potential players both in Los Angeles and in contestant searches all over the country.

Cheryl Jacobs is our research coordinator, which means that she comes up with the bulk of the puzzles, about two hundred every two weeks. Some ideas are submitted by staff members, Pat, Merv Griffin, and me. Unfortunately, regulations forbid us from accepting puzzles from outside sources, so if you think you've got some great ideas for puzzles, save your postage. We cannot even look at them.

Cheryl works with a dictionary and a thesaurus

and comes up with ideas from all over the place. Then she submits her collection of puzzle suggestions to Nancy on 3 × 5 index cards. Nancy and Merv choose which ones will be used, and these are then put into a file, with such information as what show that particular puzzle was used on, the date the show aired, and any other relevant information. For our nighttime show, puzzles are used only once, but on the daytime show, a puzzle may be used up to three times over the life of the show.

When it's time to tape the shows, Cheryl becomes the keeper of the board. She supervises the two people who change the puzzle board by hand between rounds. All of this is done in a walled-off area that no one except those three people and I have access to. Contrary to popular belief, there are no little tiny letters on the sides of the puzzle squares to help me find them. I do it all from memory and the help of backstage technicians who light up the letters as the players call them. Even though I know where the letters are, I never turn a letter before it's lit. Pat has the solution on an index card. Also, as a player calls out a letter, a woman named Robin Kenner sits under the camera Pat looks into and nods yes or shakes her head no to indicate if the letter's on the board. Then Pat will say, "No, there are no *t*'s," or whatever. Of course, Pat knows what's on the board, but this is just another of the many double-check systems we have to keep things running smoothly. Also, when players call out a letter, it is marked off on a blackboard that they can easily see. This is the famous used-letter board that Pat refers to often. This keeps someone from accidentally calling for a letter that's been called before.

To ensure that the game is played fairly and that every player has the same chance to win, each taping is watched over by at least one member of the Compliances and Practices department. The C&P department, and ones like it at all the networks, were established after it was discovered that several game shows in the fifties were rigged. These people are impartial judges. It is their duty to see that each game is played strictly by the rules and that the prizes are awarded correctly. They also make sure that all decisions made are consistent. In other words, if we have an established procedure for handling a particular problem, we must use that solution every time the problem arises.

If, for example, someone in the studio audience blurts out the answer to a puzzle, we have an established way to deal with the problem. At the start of each taping, the studio audience is requested not to talk during the rounds and told that if anyone is heard saying the answer, the taping will have to be stopped and the round started over again with a new puzzle. When this happens, all the money accumulated by the contestants in the "ruined" round is lost too, and everybody starts the new round with no money. The vast majority of audience members comply with that, but there have been cases where someone blurts the answer out. Usually these people don't mean to cause any harm. They just get so excited that they don't even realize that they're saying the answer aloud. Throughout the audience, there are C&P people who are listening for "blurts" and who will stop the taping if they hear one even if none of the contestants—or anyone else, for that matter—heard it.

In another situation, which is rare, a contestant may have meant to say, or thought she did say, one thing when in fact she said something totally different. Sometimes contestants do get that nervous. If this occurs, we play back the tape, and someone from C&P makes the final decision. There are very rarely any disputes, since it's all on tape, and tape doesn't lie.

A C&P person is also present during all steps of contestant preparation, including a briefing on the rules and strategy of the game, the rules of eligibility, and the presentation by the representative of the prize company, who explains the different prizes that will be offered and the special rules or conditions governing their delivery.

Ultimately, it is impossible to cheat at *Wheel of Fortune*. The screening process (more about that later) is very rigorous, and once contestants get to the taping, they are secluded from everyone else except the other contestants and their assigned contestant coordinator, who goes everywhere—even to the restroom—with the contestant. (Because we tape five different shows in one day, there are usually fifteen contestants and two alternates on hand each day.) Even between takes on the show, as the puzzle board is wheeled into a separate walled-off area over forty feet from the players, they must turn their backs and may look at and talk to only their contestant coordinator. Some contestants are disappointed to find that they are not allowed to talk to Pat or me before the show, not even to say hello. Of course, this is all done to ensure that everyone has an equal chance to win.

I know that people who watch the show wonder if it's not possible to spin the wheel so that it lands where you want it to. It just can't be done. For one thing, you can't just give the wheel a little baby spin when you're close to a big-money spot. It's not allowed. Second, contestants even have to do a "spin" practice, and a good hearty push is required, and that's not as easy as it looks. The wheel is quite heavy.

And just where do we get all the merchandise that we give away? From many different sources. Some prizes are given to the show, and the manufacturer pays the show a fee each time a player buys that item and Jack Clark reads its description (which cannot exceed twenty-three words). These fee spots, as they are called, help provide the funds necessary to purchase the more expensive items, like boats, cars, and vacations. The fee spots are a great way for manufacturers to advertise their products. A company called

Pic-TV coordinates the prizes and acts as a liaison between the suppliers and the show's producers.

Once a contestant wins a prize, he gets a receipt. There are a few rare exceptions to this procedure. For instance, you might get to wear a fur coat home. Ordinarily, the prize is delivered to the winner within ninety days of the show's broadcast date (usually several weeks after the taping). Different prizes are handled differently. In the case of a car, the winner would go to a dealer near where he lives, choose the color he wants, and drive it away. If the winner decides that he wants other options on the car that were not included in the prize, he may get them but at an extra cost to him. Exchanges are not permitted, although contestants can forfeit prizes that they do not want. In the case of forfeiture, there are no substitutions. The only time substitutions are allowed is when the prize firm or the manufacturer is out of stock on a specific model or it is otherwise not available. In those cases, the supplier must provide the player with a prize of equal or greater value.

Another thing I'm asked about quite often and something we've all taken some flak about is the prices of the prizes. First, we use the manufacturer's suggested retail price, which is set by the manufacturer, not anyone at *Wheel of Fortune*. If some of those seem higher than what you see in discount stores, it's because the store itself has decided to cut their profit margin on that item.

Another frequently asked question is, "If you win something, do you have to pay taxes on it?" Sorry to say, the answer is yes. As far as the government is concerned, prizes are income, so at the end of the calendar year, the prize company furnishes the contestant and the IRS with a Form 1099 (Miscellaneous Income) to anyone who won more than six hundred dollars in cash and/or merchandise. A player who wins twenty thousand dollars in prizes owes several thousand dollars in income tax. In addition, residents who live outside California must pay the California state income tax before their prizes are delivered to them.

Of course, not everyone can be a winner, and those contestants who don't win any rounds get parting gifts, which can include such things as cases of tuna, shampoo, Rice-a-Roni, hardware, motor oil, hair care products, and just about anything else.

Before the taping starts, our announcer, Jack Clark, who's been with the show longer than I, is "warming up" the audience. There are two audiences of two hundred people each day; one group sees the first set of shows, and the other sees the second set (usually two or three) that we tape after our dinner break. The stage managers brief me on the prizes that will be displayed in the opening montage. If we have time, Jack will introduce me and I'll take questions from the audience. These are usually pretty predictable questions about my wardrobe and little things about the show. I've been asked what I think about

Ed Grimley, the Martin Short character who's supposed to worship Pat Sajak, and how much money I earn. One man asked if I was single. When I replied yes, but that I lived with two cats and fifteen fish, he asked, "Can I bring my fish over to meet your fish?" Then after a few minutes, a stage manager will announce that it's time for the taping to start. When he says "Places," Jack retreats offstage to his announcer's booth, and I take my place at center stage for the opening.

When we're all in position, the overhead TV monitors in the studio show the spinning wheel as a pre-recorded crowd chants *"Wheel of Fortune!"* Next, Jack Clark invites the audience to "look at this studio, filled with glamorous prizes, fabulous and exciting merchandise" that can be won. All during this segment, I'm racing about the stage to take my place beside the next prize that I must show off. I have to watch the cues very carefully so that the camera doesn't catch me between prizes. Once the top prizes—the cars, furniture, vacations, jewelry—have all been shown, I disappear behind a curtain as Jack introduces Pat Sajak.

Then comes my introduction, for which I will be forever grateful, as Pat says the two words that have since been immortalized on a California license plate (not mine!): "Oh, Vanna." At that, the curtain is pulled and I make my entrance. Informal surveys reveal that lots of people tune in to see what I'll wear. I used to spin around every time, but now, on Merv's advice, I turn only when my dress has an interesting back or some special detail.

While Pat's introducing the three contestants and asking them about themselves, I'm back in the cordoned-off area flattening the letters on the puzzle board. This is just one more precaution we take to make sure that the players cannot possibly catch a glimpse of the letters while the board is in motion. The puzzle letters for the first round are already up on the board. The puzzle board is actually quite large—twelve feet, ten inches high and twenty-five feet, two inches long—and it rides on wheels about three feet off the ground, kind of like a small parade float. I hop aboard and three stagehands push the thing out on the stage. When the board finally stops, it's about forty feet away from the players. Then the game begins.

I think of my job as that of a cheerleader. I really do wish that everyone could be on the show and that everyone could win. I try to give the players inspiration, because I think that it's important that every contestant we have on the program has a great time, whether they win or lose. Of course, as you know, my main job is turning the letters. Merv says that he hired me because I turned the letters better than any of the two hundred other women who auditioned. And what's my secret? As I told *60 Minutes*, "It must be in the wrist!"

During a round, I concentrate and listen very carefully to what each player says. Even though I do not turn letters until they are lit up on the board, I know where each one is located, so I'm always ready to move and always know just where I'm going. When there's a long puzzle—a phrase such as "Lightning never strikes twice in the same place"—I have to rush like crazy to turn all the letters once the puzzle's been solved so Pat can get on to the next part of the game. Someone in *Time* magazine once compared my job to that of a "ball boy at a tennis match," whose responsibility it is to run onto the court closest to where the ball has come to rest. I think that just about sums it all up. Sure, it's not the most intellectually challenging job in the world—few jobs are. But it is hard work. After the prizes for that round are chosen, a new puzzle board is put together, and the wheel denominations are changed by removing one set of semicircular plywood wheels and replacing them with another set.

More often than not, our tapings go without a hitch and each half-hour game takes only about thirty-five to forty minutes to tape. Once a show is over, and Pat and I have had a chance to say good-bye to the home audience, he and I go to our respective dressing rooms and change for the next show. Pat puts on a different jacket, tie, and shirt, while I get a new dress, new hairstyle, new shoes, new accessories, and my makeup is freshened. This is when I really feel like a Barbie doll. These between-show breaks, during which technical problems are straightened out and the prizes are changed, are sometimes as long as twenty minutes. If we have a few extra minutes, I'll take some more questions and give autographs to people in the audience.

Basically, one show is very much like the rest, but in fact, there's enough about each that's different to keep it interesting. We never know what's going to happen next. The puzzles are, obviously, different, the contestants are different, and there's always the wheel. You just never know. Of course, there have been some really interesting incidents. Once, during my first season on the show, I fell flat on my face while the cameras were rolling. A contestant had just won a new Mustang, and as I stepped down off the puzzle board, I fell. I jumped up, dusted myself off, and walked over to congratulate the winner. As I approached Pat, he had a look on his face that was unforgettable, a mixture of concern and horror. When the contestant quipped, "Did you have a nice trip?" I was so embarrassed.

Another time, I'd just finished turning a letter, and as I moved off to the side, my foot grazed one of the big light bulbs, causing it to shatter. It sounded like someone had thrown a rock through a plate-glass window. I didn't dare look down until I knew the camera was off me, certain that my foot was ruined. In television, time is money, so we try to keep going even if something happens, unless our director, Dick Carson, tells us to stop. Once, while turning the letters in the middle of a round, my belt broke and nearly fell off, but I just held on to it and kept flipping those panels. After the round ended, my dresser, Florence, fixed the belt by pinning it to my dress. (Not surprisingly, this occurred during a game that was taped after the dinner break.) I've also broken fingernails, lost earrings, even stumbled.

One of the best parts of working on the show is working with Pat. In the beginning, I was always so nervous, but over time, Pat's really helped by encouraging me to ad lib. I now have much more confidence about speaking in public and doing interviews, and I have to thank Pat for a lot of that. Pat also makes it a lot of fun. Once, on Valentine's Day I gave him a heart, and he reciprocated by handing me a plastic pancreas. Another time, when we were doing a theme week—"battle of the sexes"—I playfully hit him before the last commercial break and he never got up until after the show was over. We've also played our own jokes, like the April Fool's Day when we announced that we were getting married. Of course, we were careful to end the show by saying, "April Fool's!" and laughing, but a lot of people didn't get the joke. We were deluged with wedding gifts from all over the country, and to this day, many people still think that we are married.

Being on the show has also presented me with opportunities to do things that I'd never dreamed I'd do, like hula-hooping on national television and throwing out the first ball for the Cleveland Indians (Pat did that, too).

On those rare days when everything that could go

wrong does, we try to make the best of it. Usually delays are caused by technical problems, but once we were held up when someone in the audience called out an answer. To pass the time, Pat and I went into this huge dollhouse, which was one of the prizes, and clowned around. Pat also refused to come out. The studio audience loved it. They also appreciated the fact that Pat sent out for sixteen extra large pizzas and fed the entire audience.

Another time, when an electrical failure on the puzzle board stopped the taping, Pat decided to take up residence in one of the prize platforms called the Family Room. He motioned for me join him on the expensive sofa. I sat down, then as the platform began to rotate so that the audience couldn't see us, Pat began yelling, "Vanna, stop that!"

Of course, not everything that goes wrong is funny, especially when it involves contestants. In one heartbreaking incident, a contestant had amassed the incredible sum of sixty-two thousand dollars after landing on the five-thousand-dollar spot several times. The puzzle was the phrase "The thrill of victory and the agony of the defeat." Of the forty letters, only the *v*, *c*, *l*'s, and a couple of vowels were still hidden. She called out a wrong letter, and the whole audience groaned. The next player, who had not collected very much money, solved the puzzle. But what a shame for this woman, who had a then record-breaking total (as of this writing the largest winner won sixty-five thousand dollars, which included a fifty-thousand-dollar replica of a thirties sports car). Later she told us that she'd never heard of the expression.

There was a contestant who guessed "More fun than a barrel of *Vikings*," instead of the correct *monkeys*. And another player decided to take a crack at "l _ ttery t _ _ _ et" and called out "lottery *toilet*," instead of *ticket*. Then there are those people who really luck out, like the guy whose car broke down while he was driving to Los Angeles from Arizona. He won a brand-new Corvette.

Like I did for years, you probably play the game at home and say to yourself, "Hey, I'm pretty good at this. It seems pretty simple. Why don't they just say the answer?" But it's not as easy as it looks. Being on TV is hard, knowing everyone in your town will probably be watching and that if you goof up or make a fool of yourself, everyone will know it (and most likely have it on videotape to play back for years to come). Most people get nervous just at the thought of standing up and speaking before twenty people. Imagine how it feels to stand up before forty-three million.

Most contestants fare pretty well, but there are exceptions. One classic case of freezing up was a woman who was so overwhelmed by the whole experience that she didn't even know she was winning. Her opponents were having the worst luck, while she kept landing on the big money and making the right guesses. After she'd won a round and Jack Clark was describing her prizes, she leaned over to Pat and said, "I don't know where I am!" Still, that didn't keep her from winning even more.

It seems like everyone wants to be on *Wheel of Fortune*. So far, the show's awarded millions of dollars worth of prizes to contestants. Why not you? We get our contestants by holding contestant searches all over the country. Also, if you know that you're going to be in Los Angeles, you can call us at 213-520-5555 to set up an appointment to audition. Keep in mind, however, that even if you pass the audition, you may not be on the show for several months. If you know when you'll be in the Los Angeles area, you can send a postcard to us, letting us know when you'll be in town, and an audition can be scheduled. Send it to Wheel of Fortune Contestants, 1541 North Vine Street, Hollywood, California 90028.

You'll know when we're going to visit your city when your local station announces it during one of the show's commercial breaks. A phone number is flashed, and the first eight hundred to one thousand callers get appointments to show up at a designated place, usually the ballroom of a local hotel, for the testing process. Several members of the staff, usually including producer Nancy Jones and contestant coordinators Harv Selsby and Peggy Lavell, start the two- to three-day selection process.

First the crowd is divided into smaller groups of about 125 to 150 people and given a written test, which consists of fifteen partially filled-in puzzles.

They have only five minutes to complete the test, and only those who get at least eight puzzles correct will go on to the second part of the tryouts. Usually only about thirty percent pass the written test. I wasn't nervous when I took the test, and I didn't pass. Of course, Pat took it too and scored 100!

Those who do pass move up to new seats, eight across, and are asked to call out their names so that the staff can make up a seating chart. This is where the real scrutiny begins. Nancy and the contestant coordinators are looking for several things. They're taking note of whether they can hear the person, whether the person is looking at them or staring at the floor, how clearly the person speaks, and so on. Next they all play a mock *Wheel of Fortune* game on a blackboard, with everyone in the room getting a chance to choose letters. Now Nancy watches to see if the players have their letters ready to call out when their turn comes and listens to make sure each letter is spoken distinctly.

Even at this early stage, it's pretty clear who the best players are and who is likely to crack under pressure. Then each is asked to stand up and tell a little about himself. Nancy and the contestant coordinators then go to another room and discuss the potential contestants. When they return, Nancy reads off the names of those who have "passed"—again about thirty percent—and they are asked to come back the following day to the same location for a few intense hours of game playing. In general, Nancy and the staff look for, in Nancy's words, "people the audience would want to have in their home. We look for warm, outgoing, open, friendly people who are not afraid to share with us their enthusiasm when they win or their disappointment when they lose. They need not be pretty, but they should have personality and style." The best piece of advice I can give you is just be yourself.

People are also advised on the eligibility requirements. You must be eighteen years old (except during Teen Week where the players are between thirteen and eighteen), not be related to anyone employed by NBC, RCA, GE, CBS, ABC, Merv Griffin Enterprises, or Coca-Cola, and you can appear on only one game show a year and on no more than three game shows in your entire life. But keep in mind, you can try out to be on the show as many times as you like. Some of our contestants had to try out several times before they were selected. In the end, though, only about five percent of all the people who get an initial appointment and take the written test will make it onto the show. If you do make it, you'll have a year to accept the invitation and come to Los Angeles. Of course, you must pay all of your own expenses. If you're interested in seeing the show being taped, you can send a postcard to Wheel of Fortune Tickets, c/o NBC, 3000 West Alameda Avenue, Burbank, California 91523.

Usually Pat and I are in the city where the contestant searches are under way. While Nancy and the staff are screening potential contestants, Pat and I are busy doing radio, print, and television interviews, promotional appearances, and other duties related to the show. (I'd also like to add that Pat and I have no say in who is picked to be a contestant. Several people have called me in my hotel room to plead their cases, all to no avail.) These trips are always exciting, especially when Nancy announces us and we make a surprise visit to people during the testing phase. We answer some questions, sign some autographs, and give out door prizes. It's lots of fun.

Some of the funniest things have happened to me on these promotional tours. Once I had to stand outside in subfreezing weather in an evening gown to tape a spot for the Detroit affiliate. For a southern girl who lives in California, this was torture. Tears were running down my cheeks, but I just smiled my head off.

Another time, Pat and I were in Columbus, Ohio, doing a promotion for the new nighttime show. The idea was that we would go all over town and shoot the spots at different locations. I was, of course, in the most glamorous (which usually means *hot*—as in sweltering, not sexy) gown, and Pat had on a nice three-piece suit. It was over one hundred degrees, and we spent three hours melting in the hot sun. Finally when this grueling task was all over, the station people offered to take us "anywhere" for lunch. And what establishment did Pat and I ask to be taken to? White Castle.

It was around lunchtime when our limo pulled up in front of a packed White Castle. Pat and I, dressed like we were on our way to a hot night out, jumped out of the car, went in, ordered a bagful of their thirty-cent hamburgers, then jumped back in the car and zoomed off. People must have thought they were hallucinating.

Now that *Wheel of Fortune* has become an enormous success, everybody from columnists to reporters to sociologists have tried to explain it, but nobody really can. It seems to me that the fact that it's just a great, fun, family game that everyone can play should be all the explanation anybody needs. But in the end, the real reason for our success is that you all watch it. Thanks!

worked there. At this point he was no longer working on *The Young and the Restless.* Deep down, I was happy that he decided to stop, not only for me but because the dancing was beginning to taint his image in the eyes of casting directors. John was afraid of being typecast as a "male stripper." But even if he had decided to stay with Chippendale's, I would have supported him. That's the way John and I were, always bolstering each other's self-confidence and supporting whatever the other decided to do. If one of us was happy and satisfied with what we were doing, the other was happy. It was a very unselfish love.

By the fall of 1983 things seemed secure, and I decided that it was time to buy a home. Our apartment was getting too small, and owning my own home was always a dream. Around this time John and I started talking about marriage, as we would over the coming years, always coming to the same conclusion: We would marry when we decided to have children, which we could see doing five or six years down the road. Just about the time I started looking for a house, John got an offer to appear on another soap, *One Life to Live,* as Hawk. He'd been off the first show for about a year and was anxious to get back to work. The main drawback to the job was that the show taped in New York City, not L.A. Though we still loved each other, like most couples, we had had our difficult times too. Things seemed to have reached a turning point just when the job in

New York came through, and so John moved back East. Perhaps putting some distance between us for a while was the right thing to do. He sublet an apartment in Greenwich Village, and I flew to New York to visit him as often as my schedule allowed.

One of my favorite memories of John is of the holidays in 1983. I arrived on Christmas Eve and stayed with John for two weeks, and it was heaven. He picked me up at the airport in a limousine, and we drank champagne all the way from the airport to the Village. On Christmas Day, we dined in the Crystal Room at Tavern on the Green in Central Park. It was so romantic, with the freshly fallen snow and millions of tiny icicles hanging from the bare trees. Everything was white and fresh and beautiful. It was the prettiest Christmas of my life. During those fourteen days we realized that we were meant for each other, and we renewed our commitment to our relationship.

Back in Los Angeles, I plunged back into work on *Wheel* and my other ventures, while continuing to look for a house. I was beginning to get a bit discouraged, as nothing I looked at was right. I'd always lived in dark houses, so I envisioned my new home as being very light and modern, with clean, straight lines and large, open rooms. I'd always liked the contemporary, Santa Fe–style houses I'd seen in New Mexico. But everything I saw was either out of my price range or in the wrong style.

As it happened, the house I did buy I found almost

by accident. I was driving through the Hollywood Hills one afternoon when I saw this wonderful big house perched up on a corner. I fell in love with it, so I called my real estate broker and said, "I think I've found my house!" When I described it to him, he initially thought it was another house down the street, but when he realized which one I meant, he found out that it was in foreclosure and that the bank had possession. A couple of days later, he took me inside, and it was everything I thought it would be, open and big and just beautiful! There was a fireplace, very high ceilings, an immense master bath, and windows everywhere. I called John in New York to tell him all about it. He felt a little left out, but I knew I had to make my decision soon, since other people were bidding on the house too and it was quite a bargain. Of course, there were the usual hassles and all the paperwork and extra expenses of closing, but in the end, it was mine. I moved in on June 28, 1984.

When John came back from New York after fulfilling his contract six months later, he moved into the house. He loved it and was happy just puttering around, building this, fixing that. He was such an accomplished carpenter and all-around handy person that having a real house was a great joy to him. John had always been the kind of person who wanted to do things that were "real," and building suited him perfectly.

It was around this time that his interest in show

business began to wane. He never liked the uncertainty of it all, never knowing where the next job would come from. He could have returned to Chippendale's and worked there for several more years. He always kept himself in such impeccable shape, he probably could have danced into his fifties. But that didn't really appeal to him, either. He went out on interviews and auditions regularly, mostly for TV shows and commercials, but nothing was happening, and I could see that his heart just wasn't in it. The enthusiasm was gone, and he came to think of show business as just a job. If there's one thing I know, it's that you can never look at show business as just a job. It takes too much out of you; you really have to love it.

John had many friends who later became my friends as well. One was Sondra Theodore, who later married Ray Manzella. John and Ray became friends in 1982, and they did things together, such as going skiing at Big Bear in California. The four of us had much in common, so we went out and became very close. Ray was also a great businessman and, most important, someone whose judgment I really trusted. By the time late 1985 rolled around, things were really booming for *Wheel of Fortune*. Suddenly I was a celebrity, and I found myself being asked to make all kinds of business decisions. At that time, I had an agent but not a manager. On New Year's Eve 1985, I talked to Ray about possibly managing me. I said, "I've always really wanted to do a poster. If you can get me a poster, we'll have a deal." To say that things with Ray worked out beautifully would be a real understatement. So far, getting me that poster has been the smallest thing that's happened.

Everything seemed to be looking up. John had another friend, Noel Blanc (the son of Mel Blanc, the famous voice of countless cartoon characters), who loved to fly. Noel talked about flying a lot; it was his passion. The more he talked about it, the more interested John became in the idea of flying. Noel was a helicopter pilot, and one day he took John up in his chopper. After that first time, the two of them went up about twice a week. John started taking flying lessons and became very good very quickly. In fact, he got his private, commercial, and instructor's licenses all within one year of starting lessons.

On a whim, John and Noel would take off on little adventures. One day they flew over to the Mojave Desert where Kirk Douglas was filming a movie. After they stayed a couple of hours for lunch, they offered Kirk's wife, Ann, a ride back to Palm Springs, where she was staying. John would also go with Noel on helicopter tours of the coastline. They would fly over Beverly Hills and West Los Angeles and wave to their friends. Sometimes I'd be in the house and hear a buzzing sound. I'd run outside and there would be Noel and John hovering over the backyard, "saying" hello. They'd go up to Malibu and have lunch at the Santa Barbara airport. I went with them a few times, although I was never thrilled about going up in a helicopter or any small plane. One of the nicest parts of a trip up the coast was seeing the porpoises, whales, and seals as they swam along the coast. It was always the most beautiful sight, and something John always looked forward to seeing. After he'd spotted porpoises, for example, he'd talk about them for hours. He loved them.

Before long, flying had totally consumed John. He'd still go on interviews and auditions, but he lived for the days when he could drive over to Van Nuys Airport and rent a helicopter or a small plane like the two-seat French-made Trinidad TB-20 he loved so much. On Saturday, May 17, 1986, he planned to fly up to Big Bear Lake, a mountain resort community that's about a two-hour drive from L.A. Noel had a house right on the lake, and we'd often go up there in the winter to ski. It was one of John's favorite places, probably because it reminded him so much of his hometown of Lewiston, Michigan. Since I had to work that day, he decided to take a quick trip up there by himself and have lunch.

The night before, we stayed up until one-thirty in the morning, watching one of our favorite movies on TV. Usually, we both were in bed by eleven. John liked to get up very early; sometimes he'd be in the garage working with his power tools by six. We were sitting at the breakfast table in the kitchen, having coffee, which we did every day. John was reading *USA Today*, and I was trying to wake myself up, since I had to be at NBC a few hours earlier than usual.

Dick Carson's daughter was getting married later that day, so the schedule had been rearranged to accommodate that. We were scheduled to finish at around four-thirty, which was perfect, since there was an NBC affiliates' party that night at the Playboy Mansion West, which John and I were looking forward to. John and I were both friends of Hugh Hefner's. We spent lots of time at the mansion, watching movies, lying around the pool, playing billiards, and just relaxing. I have many fond memories of times spent there. I reminded John that we had to be there at seven-thirty, and that a limousine would be by to pick us up at around seven. As I went upstairs to take my shower, I heard John leave for the airport.

The taping went smoothly, and I made my ten-minute drive back to the house, expecting to see John's red '69 Firebird parked in the driveway. When I didn't see the car, I decided to stop by my neighbors Rex and Cathi's house to say hello. I hadn't seen them in a while. Rex and I were sitting in their living room with the television on when I heard the Channel 4 newsman announce, "Man killed in plane crash at Van Nuys Airport. Details at six." It was just a bulletin, so there were no other details. I turned in the direction of the television, and for one brief, chilling moment I thought that it could have been John's plane that crashed. I felt sick to my stomach and couldn't stop thinking about it, so I asked if I could use their phone. I dialed the airport countless times, but the line was always busy. The more I dialed, the more convinced I became that John had crashed. I began to shake. Rex tried to comfort me. "It's not John, Vanna. Don't worry; calm down." But I couldn't. I excused myself and went home at five-thirty.

I drew myself a bath, all the while dialing the airport from the bathroom phone. I cursed the damn busy signal. I stepped into the tub and began to feel better instantly. I thought about John—not about the possibility that his plane had crashed at Van Nuys, but about our relationship and how much I loved him. He had been home to Michigan just a couple of weeks earlier for his twentieth high school reunion. He'd had such a great time visiting his friends, especially Mike Barnes and his wife, Carol. The week following his return had been one of the best of our relationship. Everything seemed to be perfect. We spent a lot of time together, going out to dinner at Spago's, Le Dome, and Nicky Blair's. Or we stayed at home and took baths in the Jacuzzi, which we hardly ever did. And, as always, we talked about everything.

I was startled out of my daydream by a pounding at the front door. I looked over at the clock and saw that it was 6:15. I remember thinking, "That's probably John. He forgot his keys. And look how late it is now. He has to get ready for the party." I wrapped a towel around me and bounded down the stairs to let John in, but it wasn't him. It was my neighbor, Barry Rosenblum, a doctor.

"Where is John?" Barry asked excitedly.

"He's out flying," I replied, my heart sinking with each word. "Why? What's the matter?"

"There's been an accident," Barry started to say. "Someone from the coroner's office came by my house because nobody was home here. They asked me if John Gibson lived here."

At that, I collapsed to the floor, shaking. I couldn't walk, I couldn't talk. All I could do was sit there and listen. "Why don't they know?" I asked. But Barry seemed not to hear me. He just said something about needing the name of John's dentist. "Why?" I asked.

"Because the body was burned beyond recognition, and that's the only way they can identify the person, through X rays," Barry said. Next, he phoned his wife, Abbey, to come and help him, then he went upstairs to get a robe for me to put on. It was John's robe.

All I could do was lie on the floor and think, "Maybe it's not John. He'll probably walk through the door any second and say he's sorry for being late and that he can get dressed in ten minutes for the party." There was a knock at the door. "John," I thought, "is that you?"

It was Barry's wife. While Abbey sat near me on the floor, Barry called the coroner to get more information. He learned that there had been two separate crashes that day around Van Nuys Airport. One involved six people. Then Barry called John's dentist at home. The dentist said that he'd drive over to his office right away and get the records.

The phone rang again and Barry answered, telling whoever it was to call back later. It was my best friend Annette Kizer, and when she heard Barry's unfamiliar voice, she feared that he was a burglar or that I was in some danger. When she called right back, I answered. She asked if anything was wrong, and all I could say was, "John's dead, Annette, John's dead." A second after she said she'd be right over, I collapsed. When Annette arrived a few minutes later, I was still on the den floor in hysterics. Barry said that I was in a state of shock, so he gave me a pill to sedate me. Annette sat on the floor with her arms around me. I felt so helpless. Everything had happened so quickly.

The limousine driver arrived to pick us up for the party. It was like being in a nightmare where nothing makes sense.

By that time, we'd gotten the details of the accident. The plane John had rented, the Trinidad TB-20, had gone down on Roscoe Boulevard, a busy street just north of the Van Nuys Airport runway. Amazingly, no one else was hurt. The crash had actually taken place at 3:39 that afternoon as John was attempting to make a second landing. He had successfully made one landing, but having extra time before he had to turn in the aircraft, he decided to put in a little more practice time. This was seconds after a four-engine C-130 military transport plane had touched down, creating an enormous wind turbulence with its massive wings. John didn't stand a chance; his plane just flipped over and crashed to the sidewalk. Fifteen firefighters from three engine companies fought the fire for ten minutes as John's crumpled plane lay burning against a fence. Witnesses said that they saw the small red and white plane make a nosedive, then burst into flame.

For many weeks after the crash, I questioned everyone who I thought would know: "Do you think John suffered?" That's all that was on my mind, that he didn't feel anything. When they reassured me that he hadn't suffered, it helped ease the pain.

I was still on the den floor at 7:30, facing the hardest task of my life: calling John's parents back in Michigan to tell them that their only child was dead. I picked up the receiver several times, only to hang up before I'd punched in the last digit. I was still thinking that this was all a bad dream and that I would wake up soon. At 7:35 I took a deep breath and dialed, not realizing that it was after ten in Michigan. Annette was holding on to me. The phone rang three times, then John's mother, Neva, answered. My voice was quivering as I said, "There's been an accident, Neva."

"Are you okay?" she asked. "Is John okay? What's happened?"

I choked, then I said very slowly, "There's been a plane crash, and I think John was in it."

"No, no! That's not true! Tell me it's not true. This is just a dream, right?"

"I wish to God that it was."

"Oh no, not my John, not my baby."

We both cried as she tried to tell John's father what had happened. I asked her if they could come out right away, and she promised that they would take the first plane out of Detroit the next morning. Annette made arrangements to have a car waiting for them at the airport in Los Angeles to bring them to my house.

I was able to regain my composure about a half hour later. I had other calls to make, calls that made me want to curl up and die. I phoned Mike Barnes, John's closest friend, who was also in Michigan. It was after eleven o'clock there when Mike answered the phone. "Hello, Mike," I started. "It's me, Vanna. Something's happened."

"He's dead, isn't he?" Mike said before I could even finish. He told me that he and John had talked about flying just two weeks before, at the reunion, and that he knew the minute he heard my voice that John was gone. Mike assured me that he and Carol would be on the next plane to Los Angeles. I thanked him and hung up. The hardest calls were over.

Next I called Daddy, Peggy Hursey, and my brother, Chip. It was after midnight by then, and everyone except Chip was asleep. But I couldn't wait until morning. I knew I had to release this pain. I phoned Pat Sajak and some other close friends. Everyone offered to help. I realized how wonderful my friends were. At that point, Nancy Jones came to the door.

She had been at Dick Carson's daughter's wedding when she heard the news, so she left the reception early and came to see if there was anything she could do. As we sat together, I realized that I had to tape five more shows the next day, and I knew I couldn't do it. Nancy told me not to worry about it, and the next day Susan Stafford stepped in for the Sunday tapings.

When Nancy left, I managed to get on my feet. Annette was there with me. Since coming down the stairs to answer Barry's knock early that day, I had not stood up. After four hours, my legs were like rubber. But I knew I had to get hold of myself. Silently, I walked from room to room, looking everything over carefully. I was overwhelmed by memories of the times John and I spent there over the last two years. I picked up some mementos and held them tightly. My heart hurt. I cried out, "Why couldn't it have been me, God?"

I didn't sleep that night. I certainly did not want to go to bed in our bedroom, so I lay down on the living room sofa. Annette stayed with me that night and for many days thereafter. It was still dark out when I went onto my patio and sat, waiting for the sun to come up. I was still wearing John's robe, and I buried my face in it, breathing in his aroma. I watched the birds hover over the hillside, singing their morning serenade. Annette came out to see if I was all right, but I just wanted to be alone with my thoughts. I felt very close to John that morning. It was as if he were telling me that he was safe and not in pain.

The phone started ringing at seven and didn't stop for days. Flowers, cards, letters, food, and fruit baskets poured in. Thousands of *Wheel of Fortune* fans sent letters and cards expressing their sympathy. A small boy from Plymouth, Massachusetts, was watching the news with his mother when he heard about John's accident. His mother wrote, saying that little Jeremy cried his eyes out and said, "I should go and keep Vannie company, so she wouldn't be so sad. I'll come back home when she's happy again." Enclosed was Jeremy's drawing of me with a smiling face.

Late Sunday morning John's parents arrived. They had been up since midnight, having left their home during a violent rainstorm. I met them halfway up the driveway. We embraced, the three of us holding back tears. There was so much to say, but where to start?

When we got into the house and put away the suitcases, Annette fixed everyone a drink and we sat down in the living room to discuss funeral arrangements. John had told me several times that he wanted to be cremated, so we planned that and a memorial service. Annette then went home to change clothes, and by the time she returned to the house, she had all the necessary papers, and the arrangements were complete.

Leo and I had to go to the coroner's office and

pick up the personal items that were left after the crash. They gave us a small box, which reeked of smoke and ashes. Inside it were several flying manuals and John's wallet. All the money was burnt, and the credit cards were melted around the edges, though you could still make out the account numbers. The only item in his wallet that was not even singed was his favorite picture of me.

Later that week, Leo and I drove over to the Grandview Crematory in Glendale to pick up the urn that contained John's ashes. I know it might sound morbid, but I held on to that box of ashes for hours. When you know you'll never see or touch or feel someone ever again, you will do anything that makes you feel close to that person.

On Wednesday, May 21, at seven in the evening, a memorial service was held for John at the Westwood Memorial Park Chapel. I wore the black leather dress that John had given to me for my twenty-ninth birthday. Annette helped me get dressed that day. While I was pulling on a pair of stockings, I commented that John didn't like these. Just then, the stocking ran. When Annette quipped, "Well, I guess he didn't want you to wear them," I laughed for the first time since John had died.

The service was beautiful. There were so many people there that they couldn't all fit into the chapel. John had so many friends. There were flowers everywhere and large pictures of John hanging up. I sat in the first row between John's parents and Annette and her husband Tom. The minister, Reverend Robert Bock, knew John, since he was also an actor and had played a clergyman on *The Young and the Restless*. When the minister was finished with his talk, he asked Ray Manzella to say a few words in tribute. Ray said, "John Gibson died at a time in his life when he was happiest. He was happy with the lady in his life and he was doing what he loved to do the most, fly."

Next, Mike Barnes read the eulogy he had written on the plane from Michigan. Of all of us, Mike probably knew John the best; they'd been friends for more than twenty years. He said in part: "I loved John Gibson. He was my friend and for that I will always be grateful. I don't know the words to say good-bye. I only know that he is in my heart and soul. I search for an answer and there is none to find. I want to be with my friend to play an earthly game or touch a loving hand. . . . I will miss so very much—the plans, the adventures we had planned for the future—and I will hold dear the cherished memories of our past."

Then Mike looked over in my direction and continued his eulogy by saying, "Vanna, I don't think I've ever known John to be happier than the last few years he spent here with you. You are very special. John flourished with you, Vanna, and often spoke of his deep love for you. You have made his life complete."

I was holding Annette's hand so tightly, I was sure I was hurting her. I tried to hold back my tears, but it was impossible, and they streamed down my face as I recalled all the good times John and I had shared and thought of how much I would miss him.

The ceremony ended and the Gibsons and I stood up by our pew in the chapel and spoke briefly to the few hundred people who were there. Forty-five minutes later, a few of us went up to Annette's house for a quiet meal.

The first few days after the service seemed to be very long. With Leo, Neva, Mike, and Carol there, I felt stronger. Even though John and I never married, there was a bond between the Gibsons and me. To this day I talk on the phone with them at least once a week. When John was alive, they would take their vacations out here. And every summer John and I would go to Michigan and spend two weeks on the lake, just fishing and having a great time.

On Memorial Day Noel Blanc took Leo and Neva up in his helicopter. I stayed at home with my friend Kathy Smith. I felt that Leo and Neva should share that time alone. Neva held the box containing John's ashes. Noel flew to John's favorite spot, just south of Oxnard. It was late morning and it was foggy near the ocean, but at the very spot John so loved, the weather was clear, not foggy.

After saying a prayer, they opened the copter door and Leo carefully sprinkled John's ashes into the ocean. At what I believe was that exact moment, I experienced a sudden feeling of peace and warmth, as if I were being somehow comforted. What I didn't know until later was that the instant John's ashes fell into the ocean, twenty or thirty porpoises came to the surface, bobbing up and down and circling the spot where the ashes had fallen, as if in a kind of greeting. How odd, Noel, Leo, and Neva thought. When they got back to the house and told me about the incident, I took them into a room where I kept a framed picture of John as a little boy, standing on a boat. Next to it was the ivory porpoise statue that John bought me during our first trip to Maui.

That night I had a dream. In it, John appeared in a gray haze. He was alone and he told me not to worry about anything. He said that he was happier than he'd ever been before, and that he was in the most beautiful place he'd ever seen. He was thankful that no one else got hurt or killed in the plane crash. But what he was most concerned about were his parents, friends, and me. He begged me to stop mourning and to tell everyone how happy he was and that there was nothing to be sad about. And I believed him. Still, he was gone.

John's parents stayed with me for another week, which was a great relief, since I didn't want to be alone in the house. The three of us put up brave fronts, for the others' sakes, but deep down we were all hurting. We pulled out photo albums and looked at them together, reminiscing about John. It was painful, but I felt like it was something we had to do.

Leo and I sorted through John's things and organized them into piles. There were things John's parents would take back with them, things I would keep, and things we'd give away to charity or to friends. This was particularly difficult, because every item— be it a piece of clothing, a letter, a souvenir, a tool —triggered off a story or a memory. There were times when we just had to stop. It was too much.

The reality for me, something that I still haven't gotten entirely used to, is that I'll never see John again. We couldn't have been closer. It seemed so strange not to have John around. And I still miss him every day.

9

♥

Six weeks before the accident, John and I had agreed to take part in the thirty-fifth annual Sun Fun Festival in North Myrtle Beach. During the festival's first few years, it attracted only a few hundred visitors; today about three hundred thousand visitors come down for it. The event's seven days are filled with planned beach games and activities, such as sand castle–building and watermelon-eating contests. And of course, there's the Miss Sun Fun beauty pageant and two parades, one in Myrtle Beach and another in North Myrtle Beach. Beginning in the seventies, various celebrities, among them Gary Sandy and Frank Bonner from *WKRP in Cincinnati*, Willard Scott, Greg

Morris, Hal Needham, and Captain Kangaroo (Bob Keesham) have participated in the festivities as grand marshals of the Sun Fun parade. In 1986 I was honored to be asked to be the grand marshal, and John agreed to appear as a special guest. He'd been back to North Myrtle Beach with me a few times over the years, and he always enjoyed meeting my friends and family and visiting my old haunts.

Immediately after John's death, I was torn between canceling or going through with it alone. My manager, Ray, had already postponed a number of things, including scheduled appearances on David Letterman's show and *Good Morning America*. If I was going to go through with Sun Fun, I was going to have to leave just four days after John's parents left Los Angeles on May 31. No one tried to pressure me one way or the other, though many of my friends in Los Angeles thought I was crazy when I said I was going. One reason I decided to go was that John would have been the first to say, "Vanna, do it." Had it been any other town or event, I wouldn't have gone, but I really needed to go home.

I phoned my contact at the Chamber of Commerce, Marilyn Chewning, and told her I would be there on Friday, June 6. I told Marilyn that I did not know the extent to which I would be able to participate, and she understood. They had a long list of activities planned for me—the parade, press conferences, autograph sessions, radio shows, press interviews, and so on.

During the flight back East, it suddenly dawned on me that I would be arriving in North Myrtle Beach and not calling John to let him know that I'd arrived safely. It's funny how little things like that make you realize what losing someone you love means. I checked into the Beach Cove Inn, made a few phone calls to friends and family, and then went to bed. The first event, the welcoming, took place at the Myrtle Beach Pavilion, followed by the human checkers game. Then came a luncheon, press interviews, more activities. The hardest part, the parades, were scheduled for the next day.

The parades went just fine, but it all seemed like a blur. It sounds like a cliché, but I really was smiling on the outside and crying on the inside. I managed to smile all the way. Everyone around me was very understanding, and very careful not to mention John's death. That night I attended a reception, and right across the hall, in another ballroom, Bonnie Baldwin, whom I used to babysit, was getting married. Seeing her was nice, and it made me feel good. At a time like that, it really struck me how quickly we all grow up, how swiftly life passes by. Seeing Bonnie just brought a flood of childhood memories, and I'd remember something very beautiful and pleasant, then begin thinking about death. I felt like I had no control over my mind at all; I just couldn't stop thinking about these things.

On Sunday, the last day of Sun Fun, my father, my stepmother Paula, and Chip hosted a picnic in our backyard. It was just like a family reunion. Daddy had married Paula several years before, and they are very happy together. He had also recently retired from the post office and is now working in real estate. It was so good just to be home. About thirty people came, and it was wonderful to be able to kick off my shoes and act silly with my cousins, aunts, and uncles.

The last event of the weekend was a reception in my honor given by the Friends of Vanna White and held at the Surf Golf and Beach Club. Although I'd done all right up to that point, I really wasn't up to this last event. I just wanted to stay at Daddy's or go back to the hotel and relax for the trip back to L.A. the next day. But I couldn't say no, and as it turned out, I was very glad that I went.

Five hundred people, some of whom I hadn't seen in ten years, showed up. All of my high school buddies, and people I'd grown up with, including my first best girlfriend, Beth Johnson, were there too. Reminiscing with everyone not only took my mind off John for those few hours, but also reminded me how much I loved my hometown and how lucky I was to have grown up around such wonderful people. They made me feel that I wasn't alone. My friends showed me in many ways that they cared for me and they were there when I needed them most. Thank you all.

When it was time to go, I said my good-byes and got into the limousine to go back to my hotel. Momma's friend Peggy Hursey was with me. I thought about how happy all my friends were, with their spouses and lovers. Of course I was happy for them, but it only reminded me that John was gone. As we pulled away from the Surf Club, I put my head on Peggy's shoulder and cried my eyes out. I was so relieved that it was all over. As grateful as I was for everyone's support, I learned that I wasn't nearly as strong as I'd hoped I was. It was a great comfort to know that I wouldn't have to put on a happy face again for a while.

On Monday, June 9, I left for Los Angeles, and my brother, Chip, came with me to keep me company. Knowing how much pain I was in, he decided he would move permanently to Los Angeles. I know how difficult it was for him to leave his friends in South Carolina, and I only hope he realizes how much his love and support have meant to me during this difficult time.

My four-week vacation from the show was almost over, and *Wheel of Fortune* was going back into production the following Monday. From the minute I got home, all I did was sleep—for the next seven days. I was so exhausted. I hadn't really slept well or rested since John's accident, and I didn't look or feel that well. I'd lost weight, and I looked and felt very tired.

It was so good just to have Chip around. There was no pressure; I didn't have to put up a front for him. If I wanted to cry, I did. If I wanted to go out to have dinner, we did that. During this week, I finally began to come to grips with the enormity of John's death and how it had changed my life. One day I might wake up and feel like I had things more or less under control; then something would happen that would remind me of the many wonderful days John and I had spent together. For example, there was the day when John's flight instructor's license came in the mail, and the times I'd see on television the commercial he'd made for the Tropicana Hotel in Las Vegas. I knew I was going to have to get used to this, but not yet. Death may be final, but its aftermath is never ending.

Going back to work was probably the best thing I could have done. When I arrived at the studio for the first day's taping, it was like I'd never been away; I got right back into the familiar routine. All my friends and co-workers had sent cards and letters to me, or spoken to me or seen me at home since John died, so they didn't have to bring up the subject. When we took our dinner break that afternoon, which was the first time that day I was able to relax, I remember having a real empty feeling inside. I caught myself looking toward the door, expecting John to suddenly walk in, grab a plate, and sit down next to me. Of course, that was not to be. But you can't always control what goes through your mind.

Ironically, *Wheel of Fortune* had peaked just a few months before. Not that the show hadn't done well before; it had. But suddenly it seemed that everyone was writing about the show or Pat or me. Looking back, it's hard to say exactly what caused this sudden publicity blitz. I didn't have a press agent out "planting" stories, and I gave relatively few interviews, especially after John died. To look at the tabloids, though, you'd think that all I did was talk to them.

The most disturbing thing was to walk into the supermarket or through an airport and see a tabloid with a headline about how I had brought John back from the grave, or how Pat Sajak and I were having a secret affair (but the show's producers forbade us to wed). It was absolutely unbelievable. It would be one thing if I thought no one ever read or believed these publications, but I know from experience that they do. These magazines made up stories and made up quotes, so it would seem that I'd talked to them, when I hadn't. Sadly, you can't sue a publication just for lying about you or making up stories unless the stories are libelous, and that's very hard and very expensive to prove. Most of the time, it's just not worth bothering about. Besides, suing such a magazine only gives them more publicity.

And, as I've also learned, there's no law against these people invading not only my privacy but that of my friends and family. By now, anyone who's known me, no matter how casually, has been harassed by reporters who call them on the phone at all hours of the night and actually turn up on their doorsteps! I've changed my unlisted phone number more times than I can count, but that doesn't stop them either. I still get calls from reporters who pretend to know me or claim to be working for a far more respectable magazine than the one they're actually with.

Of course, I understand that these people have a job to do, and I'm happy to cooperate when we all know the rules and respect each other. But imagine how I felt when we found reporters on my doorstep just hours after John's plane crashed. And tabloids aren't the only offenders. After John died, I agreed to do interviews, but always with the understanding that I would talk about anything but John. Before I'd sit for the interview, the writers would be informed of this condition and they would agree. Most writers were truly professional and did respect my wishes. But several did not. One even asked me, "So who paid the mortgage—you or John?"

Needless to say, I approached the press with a little more caution. The year before, *People* had quoted out of context something I'd said. In the course of the interview I'd said, "I'm not like those *Price Is Right* girls. I have a different function on the show. I turn the letters." What I meant was very clear: I was part of the game itself in addition to presenting the prizes. I know the women on the *The Price Is Right*, and I like them. I wasn't saying that what I did was in any way better, just different. But when the story ran, I came off sounding like a snob. The only part of the quote that ran was the first sentence: "I'm not like those *Price Is Right* girls."

I felt terrible about it. I explained it to Janice, one

of the *Price* hostesses, and she understood. Then I tried to put it into perspective for myself. After all, here was a magazine that couldn't even get my eye color right! Also, I'd made the mistake of answering their stupid questions with some stupid answers. At the moment it was all I could think to do, but when the story came out, I looked like a fool. That was the last time I did that. Interestingly, Pat had declined to be interviewed for that particular piece. I'm often asked if Pat is jealous of the media attention I've received, and the answer is no. He couldn't be more supportive of me, and because he's a very private person, he really doesn't mind not being in the public eye.

Shortly after I'd returned to work, *People* called and asked if I'd grant them an interview for a special piece they were doing. At first, I refused. From my earlier experience, I felt that I really couldn't trust them. But over the next couple of weeks, the *People* representative talked to my manager, Ray, and they came to an agreement. First, the story was supposed to be about "the ten most interesting people on television." Second, it was not to be a Vanna White cover; rather, there would be ten little pictures on the cover, one for each of the "interesting people." I was mainly concerned that it not be a full cover shot because I still didn't look very well; I was underweight and still very tired.

With these guidelines set, we proceeded to do the interview. I had dinner with the writer, posed for an at-home picture (in a friend's house, not my own) and for a glamour shot in a gown. I had a strange feeling about this whole thing, but I tried to be reasonable about it. After all, I told myself, they couldn't possibly burn me twice. Then I saw the story. There I was—taking up over half the cover—with a headline that read: "Wheel of Fortune's Vanna White and TV's Hippest Oddballs." The story made me sound like a total airhead. But worse than that was the fact that they'd lied to me and to Ray, and essentially tricked me into doing it, knowing full well that if they'd been honest with us, I wouldn't have cooperated.

Also that summer, I suffered what I thought was the ultimate invasion of privacy when a low-class "men's" magazine published photos of me topless. Did I pose topless? No! Like lots of people, I like to sunbathe—I think it's a great way to relax—and I hate tan lines. I'm also not convinced that tanning salons are totally safe either. So I sunbathe in my own private backyard. Somehow, a Peeping Tom photographer with a telephoto lens got some shots. They were taken from such a distance and had to be so grossly enlarged that you can't even really tell that it's me. But it is. And I could do nothing about it. A photograph belongs to the photographer, not the subject, and the photographer can do whatever he wants with it.

Pulling myself back together was hard enough. Having things like these happen made it seem impossible at times. But these situations pale in comparison to what came later. In 1986, *Playboy* named me one of its sex stars of 1986, along with Tom Cruise, Don Johnson, Whitney Houston, Dr. Ruth Westheimer, Bruce Willis, Brooke Shields, Kim Basinger, Rob Lowe, Heather Thomas, Jim McMahon, and Cybill Shepherd. I was flattered to be included, and that year I agreed to pose—clothed but admittedly looking sexy—in the magazine as a favor to its publisher, Hugh Hefner. Hef, as we called him, had been a friend of John, my manager, Ray, Ray's wife, and myself for years. I knew Hef as a sweet and gentle man and counted him as one of my dearest friends.

Over that summer, though, the inevitable happened: the photographer who shot those lingerie ads when I first arrived in L.A., surfaced with those pictures. As I said before, I knew from the minute I'd accepted that job that I had made a mistake, and I knew this was going to happen sooner or later. In fact, when I'd first gotten the job on *Wheel*, I told Nancy Jones that these photos existed.

The photographer offered the shots to *Playboy* and *Penthouse*, and Hef ended up buying them. When Ray and I found out about this, he tried to convince Hef to postpone their publication, at the very least, and perhaps even dissuade him from publishing them at all. I was even willing to do a *Playboy* cover and some promotion in exchange. Finally it was agreed that they would be postponed.

Although the situation seemed to have been resolved for the moment, I just couldn't stop thinking about it. I was embarrassed and very upset, and the thought of seeing those photos plastered all over the country kept me awake many nights. The worst part, of course, was knowing that it was my fault, and one way or another, I was going to have to pay dearly for a very stupid mistake.

Finally, I couldn't stand it any longer, and I made an appointment to meet with Hef in person on December 8, 1986. Hef greeted me when I arrived, and we went up to his office to discuss the problem. We each explained our sides of the story, and I can honestly say that I understood that he had a magazine to run, and he understood that I had my career to protect. No matter how you cut it, neither solution was going to make both of us happy; one of us was bound to lose. But after we'd talked it over, Hef said to me, "Vanna, I would never do anything to hurt you."

I replied, "Hef, this would hurt me."

"Then that's it," Hef said. "I won't run them." He then gave me a big hug, and as I left, he stood up and, crying, he said, "It's only money."

We each wiped away our tears and then went downstairs. I felt so relieved that I wrote him a note before I even left the mansion.

I drove away from the mansion believing that I had a true friend who would honor his promise and not exploit another friend just to make a buck. But

I was wrong. Unfortunately, the story does not have a happy ending. A few weeks after our meeting, I received a letter from Hef saying that the matter was out of his hands and that he had to run the pictures. Not coincidentally, they were scheduled to run in the issue that comes out the same month this book is to be published. Of course, ultimately, I have to accept the responsibility for my actions. I made a terrible mistake. And I can never say it too many times: Always follow your heart. If something feels wrong, it probably is.

There was also the matter of learning to adjust to life without John, a long, ongoing process. At the end of December 1986, just weeks after the *Playboy* fiasco, I decided that it was time to go and visit John's parents. Looking back, I can see that I spent many months believing that I had everything under control. Having handled all of the business things a death involves and carrying on with my career had given me a false sense of security. I believe that when devastating things happen, something inside you takes over. We are usually much stronger in these situations than we think we will be. Nonetheless, I'd put off seeing John's parents. I suppose, deep down, I knew that I still had more healing to do than I wanted to believe. But it was time.

When I arrived in West Palm Beach, Leo and Neva met me, and we spent the next few days just doing all kinds of homey things together—eating, cooking, shopping. Of course, none of us will ever really get over losing John, but I was relieved to see the two of them in good health and basically doing so well. Those three days were wonderful, and although we all missed John, I felt his presence the whole time.

The minute I walked into my house, I went to sleep, and when I woke up at 8:30 the next morning, I felt like someone had dropped a bomb on me. It was the day of New Year's Eve, and I just kept thinking about John. I drew all the blinds, couldn't talk to anyone, and just stayed in bed all day. This was the lowest I'd ever felt in my life. I felt that nothing mattered, that I wanted to run away from everyone and everything.

By that evening I was still feeling the same way, but Chip talked me into going to a New Year's Eve party with him. I didn't want to, but I knew that if I didn't I'd just sit around feeling miserable. As it turned out, going to the party was the best thing I could have done. Many of my friends were there, and once again I saw that even though things may seem hopeless, they really never are. There are always people around to help you if you just let them. After that party, I felt more optimistic about the new year than ever. Of course, I know there will be other rough times ahead. The key is to keep things in perspective.

But then there's the bright side of my life, and there's enough good to outweigh the bad. One of the best parts is getting to meet and work with nice people, like Pat and the other people on the show. Another aspect is actually getting to do the things I'd dreamed about for years. Being on Johnny Carson's *Tonight* show is right at the top of the list. For some reason, I'm nervous every time I do a talk show. It's not like I play a role on television and then have to come on a talk show and reveal the "true" me. I'm always the same person, so it can't be that. But it must be something. Before the Carson show, I agonized for days over what I would wear, what he would say, what I would say, and on and on. Two friends designed a gorgeous royal blue and silver beaded gown for me to wear on the occasion. The two of them, my manager, Ray, some friends from NBC, and a couple of fans who've seen every taping of *Wheel* I've appeared on went with me for moral support.

But even with all those familiar faces and my makeup man Bruce there, I was pacing the tiny dressing room, with a million thoughts running through my mind. I was to go on last, right after opera star Luciano Pavarotti. As the stage manager came to get me during the commercial break, I froze. Everyone there wished me good luck, and I waited in the wings for my introduction. I took a deep breath, and when I heard Johnny say my name, I walked out through the curtains, waved hello, walked toward him, and took my seat. This was really it. The only thing I remember is Johnny saying to me, "I hear you don't like three things—liver, lamb, and opera."

By the time he got to the word *things*, I knew exactly what was coming. This was one of those quotes I'd given to the press. But here I was sitting next to Pavarotti, probably the greatest living opera singer in the world. For a moment I froze, but then Mr. Pavarotti came to my rescue by saying, "I don't like liver or lamb, and perhaps tonight I don't like opera either." How sweet of him! I grabbed his hand and told him how wonderful he was, and the next day I bought some of his albums. And after listening to them, I've decided that I do like opera, after all.

When it was all over, I went back to my dressing room to change, and everyone congratulated me on what a great job I'd done. I was still in shock. It's funny to think that something I'd dreamed about doing for so many years finally happened, and here I couldn't remember a thing about one of my fondest memories!

Another thrill was being invited to appear on the first of Garry Shandling's Showtime specials. It was July 1986 and I still wasn't totally recovered from John's death, but I wanted to do it. Ray was able to reschedule some other things, so I could. Although I was just playing myself doing what I do on the show, this was very different. For a sketch called "The Day Garry Moved In," the show's set designer had made a replica of the *Wheel* puzzle board that was incredibly precise. All the action occurred in a dream sequence, and in the end the puzzle board reveals that "I [me] stole Garry Shandling's furniture." It was the craziest skit, and I didn't know quite where it was all leading until I saw the show broadcast a few weeks later.

I also played myself on Jay Leno's special, although this time the solution to the board's puzzle wasn't made up of letters but symbols, like eyes and lettuce, that spelled out the show's mystery—that Jay Leno had killed David Letterman.

Once Pat was a guest on David Letterman's show. While Pat was on, I was waiting backstage in the green room. Following his segment, David decided to come back and get me, all on camera. They found me, and right before they broke for the commercial, David pinched me on the bottom. Now, I know that this is not the way the word is used by everyone today, but back when I was young, we called this kind of pinch a "goose." At that moment, there wasn't much I could do, but I patiently waited, and a few months later I got my chance. I was invited to be on his show again, so I brought along a very nicely wrapped present. When I got to the studio, the producer informed me that David really didn't like getting surprise presents on the air, so I went back to my dressing room, unwrapped the gift, and very carefully stuffed it down the back of my outfit. Of course, I was my usual nervous self, but at the end of my segment—which is aired live—I pulled out the gift and presented it to David. It was a T-shirt that said, "I goosed Vanna

White." Since then, I've gotten countless requests from people who want copies of that shirt. Sorry, guys, it's one of a kind!

It's been great fun working with people such as Garry Shandling, Jay Leno, and David Letterman. I even enjoy being a subject of Joan Rivers's jokes. Sure, some of them are a bit catty, but that's her style, so it doesn't bother me. I know that I'm the perfect target for potshots and kidding, and I don't even mind criticism as long as it's done fairly. I get a kick out of hearing my name mentioned on other shows, and I even laughed when *Mad* magazine parodied the show and renamed me Vanilla Wipe. The only thing that I object to is critics who act as if I'm single-handedly responsible for the notoriety I've received. But, that's life.

Another interesting part of my new fame is being asked to do endorsements for products. I've gotten lots of offers, but I'll endorse only those products I use and believe in. I eat at McDonald's (I love their fries with lots of ketchup); I sleep on Spring Air mattresses; I eat Nestle's chocolate (probably more than I should!); and I use my Buf-Puf every day, and have for years. Working on these ads and commercials takes me back to my modeling days and is a real change of pace. I've also gotten offers for all kinds of other projects, but never fear—I have no plans to leave *Wheel of Fortune*. Because of my schedule I can usually work around it, which I would do, even if my secret dream—to be in a Woody Allen film—ever came true. I feel very fortunate to be able to say, with all sincerity, that I truly love my job.

Of course, fame always changes your personal life, sometimes in ways that aren't good. I try to live as normally as possible, but now when I go to the supermarket, people will follow me, which is innocent enough. But other times, it can be frightening. I've gotten some very upsetting phone calls and messages; I've also been followed by strangers while I'm driving in my car. Of course, these incidents are always reported to the proper authorities, but it can be very scary.

So although almost everything in my professional life has changed, some things will always be the same. I'll always want what I think is the most important thing in life—someone to share my life and have children with. Six years after I left North Myrtle Beach, I came home for the premiere of *Graduation Day*, my first film. A friend who'd been a cheerleader with me came up to ask for an autograph. I couldn't believe it, and before I even thought, I said, "Are you kidding? It's me, Vanna!" Thinking about that incident today reminds me that that's who I am— just Vanna. Sure, things sometimes happen faster than you can absorb them, but you always have to just keep going and never lose sight of who you are or your dreams. As my parents always used to say to Chip and me, "You never know, they could come true." And they do.

VANNA on growing up in a small town: "As soon as you mention that you're from a small, southern, tourist beach town, most people assume that your life was boring or that your folks were typical, small-town people. But while it's true that my childhood was pretty normal, it was anything but boring."

★ ☆ ★

VANNA on fashion: "Accessories are the key. It's a lot less expensive—and a lot more fun—to buy one great black dress and several sets of accessories— belts, shoes, bags, costume jewelry, hats, stockings, scarves. Plus you can use those accessories to expand other outfits. . . . A good wardrobe isn't a lot of clothes, it's a lot of looks."

★ ☆ ★

VANNA on those pictures in *Playboy*: "I learned an excellent lesson, one that no one should have to learn: Never, ever do something you feel uncomfortable about—no matter what the reason. I guarantee you, it will come back to haunt you."

★ ☆ ★

VANNA on the death of John Gibson: "The reality for me, something that I still haven't gotten entirely used to, is that I'll never see John again. We couldn't have been closer. It seemed so strange not to have John around. And I still miss him every day."

★ ☆ ★

VANNA on *Wheel of Fortune*: "I think of my job as that of a cheerleader. I really do wish that everyone could be on the show and that everyone could win. I try to give the players inspiration, because I think it's important that every contestant we have on the program has a great time, win or lose."

☆